5/17/11
$34.95

Western Lands and Waters Series
XXIV

Murder
of a Landscape
The California Farmer-Smelter War
1897–1916

by
Khaled J. Bloom

THE ARTHUR H. CLARK COMPANY
An imprint of the University of Oklahoma Press
Norman, Oklahoma
2010

Also by Khaled J. Bloom:

The Mississippi Valley's Great Yellow Fever Epidemic of 1878
(Baton Rouge, 1993)

Library of Congress Cataloging-in-Publication Data

Bloom, Khaled J., 1954–
    Murder of a landscape : the California farmer-smelter war, 1897–1916 / by Khaled
J. Bloom.
    p. cm. — (Western lands and waters series ; 24)
    Includes bibliographical references and index.
  ISBN 978-0-87062-396-7 (hardcover : alk. paper)
    1. Air—Pollution—California—Shasta County—History. 2. Environmental disas-
ters—California—Shasta County—History. 3. Copper smelting—Environmental as-
pects—California—Shasta County—History. 4. Farmers—California—Shasta
County—Political activity—History. 5. Social conflict—California—Shasta County—
History. 6. Desertification—California—Shasta County—History. 7. Landscape—California—Shasta County—History. 8. Shasta County (Calif.)—Environmental conditions.
9. Shasta County (Calif.)—History—19th century. 10. Shasta County (Calif.)—History—20th century. I. Title. II. Series.
    TD883.5.C2B55 2010
    363.739'209794—dc22
                                            2009047078

The California Farmer-Smelter War, 1897–1916
is Volume 24 in the Western Lands and Waters Series.

The paper in this book meets the guidelines for permanence and durability
of the Committee on Production Guidelines for Book Longevity
of the Council on Library Resources, Inc. ∞

To the memory of
James H. Shideler and Paul W. Gates,
who encouraged my first efforts in agricultural history

Contents

Illustrations

Acknowledgments

For encouragement of the work early on and along the way, I thank Nigel Allan, Conrad Bahre, Roger Byrne and gang, Bill Critchfield, Alfred Crosby, Ray Dasmann, John Easterly, Richard Eaton, Lou Grivetti, Patti Hartmann, Tomar Mason, Richard Orsi, James Parsons, Stan Trimble, and Paul Zinke.

For reference help I thank Nancy Zimmelman and others at the California State Archives, Rosemary Kennedy and others at the San Francisco branch of the National Archives, Dick Rumboltz and others at Shasta Dam, Don Westphal and others at Sacramento, Dennis Galvin and others at the old Pacific Southwest experiment station, Gary Barker and Scott Miller at Arava Natural Resources, and Ingrid Radkey, Norma Kobzina, and Beth Weil at the Bioscience and Natural Resources Library, University of California, Berkeley. Also various folks at the College Park and Kansas City branches of the National Archives, and most certainly everyone at the California History Section of the California State Library. As well as other good people at Shasta College, the Shasta Historical Society, the Bancroft Library, the Montana Historical Society, the Utah Historical Society, and the Tennessee Valley Authority. For help with the maps I thank Luke Soiu and Bill Nelson.

For critical appraisals of the work as it approached its present form, I thank Steven Baker, Phil Bansal, Michael Barbour, Bob Clark, Dennis Dingemans, Emily Jerman, Peter Lindert, Michael Magliari, Beth Mills, Duane Smith, and Jessica Walker.

Abbreviations

BR 442   Central File 442: Research, Testing, and Technical Miscellany: Sedimentation, U.S. Bureau of Reclamation, Shasta Dam, Calif.

BR 580   Central File 580: Keswick Reservoir Watersheds: April 1951–December 1957, U.S. Bureau of Reclamation, Shasta Dam, Calif.

CCA 1203   Civil Case File 1203, Ninth U.S. Circuit Court of Appeals, Record Group 276, National Archives and Records Administration–Pacific Region (San Francisco), San Bruno, Calif.

CCA 2549   Civil Case File 2549, Eighth U.S. Circuit Court of Appeals, Record Group 276, National Archives and Records Administration–Central Plains Region, Kansas City, Mo.

CSC 1847   Civil Case File 1847 (Sacramento District), California Supreme Court, California State Archives, Office of Secretary of State, Sacramento, Calif.

DOI 5154-1897 Letters Received File 5154-1897, Lands and Railroads Division, U.S. Department of the Interior, Record Group 48, National Archives at College Park, Md.

DOJ 5706-1898 Year File 5706-1898, U.S. Department of Justice, Record Group 60, National Archives at College Park, Md.

DOJ 144276   Straight Numerical File 144276, U.S. Department of Justice, Record Group 60, National Archives at College Park, Md.

FS RCF   Research Compilation File: Smelter Fumes, U.S. For-
                   est Service, Record Group 95, National Archives at
                   College Park, Md.

GLO 30   California Timber Trespass Case File 30, Special Serv-
                   ices Division, U.S. General Land Office, Record
                   Group 49, National Archives at College Park, Md.

GLO 55979   Case File 55979, Division "P," U.S. General Land Of-
                   fice, Record Group 49, National Archives at College
                   Park, Md.

NDC 12633   Civil Case File 12633, U.S. District Court for the
                   Northern District of California, Record Group 21, Na-
                   tional Archives and Records Administration–Pacific
                   Region (San Francisco), San Bruno, Calif.

NDC 15122   Civil Case File 15122, U.S. District Court for the
                   Northern District of California, Record Group 21, Na-
                   tional Archives and Records Administration–Pacific
                   Region (San Francisco), San Bruno, Calif.

NDC 15123   Civil Case File 15123, U.S. District Court for the
                   Northern District of California, Record Group 21, Na-
                   tional Archives and Records Administration–Pacific
                   Region (San Francisco), San Bruno, Calif.

Introduction

Booming demand for copper in the closing years of the nineteenth century spurred discovery and exploitation of ore deposits in many odd corners of the world. The lower Sacramento River canyon in Shasta County in northern California was one prominent focus of this activity. Rothschild capital pioneered the area in 1896, followed with large investments by a Boston syndicate in 1903 and the Guggenheims in 1905. For a few years, indeed, copper was California's most talked-about mineral product, bumping aside more storied rivals like gold and petroleum. Three large smelters were erected in Shasta County, burning thousands of tons of copper sulfide ore every week and thereby liberating thousands of tons of sulfur dioxide, a gas unpleasant to people and animals, and exquisitely fatal to plants.[1]

The mostly midwestern population that trailed into the northern end of the Sacramento Valley after 1849 had found the Mediterranean environment agreeable—summers and falls were hot and dry, but winters and springs were mild and moist enough to make farming pay, usually. Over the next half century American settlers converted the bottomlands into grain, hay, and stock ranches, while the chaparral and

---

[1] Kinkel, Hall, and Albers, *Geology and Base-Metal Deposits of West Shasta Copper-Zinc District, California*; Zimmerman, *World Resources and Industries*, 666–93; Winner, Mooney, and Goldstein, *Sulfur Dioxide and Vegetation: Physiology, Ecology, and Policy Issues*.

scrub woodland of the surrounding foothills were increasingly slashed and burned to create small but viable orchards and vineyards. The agricultural prospects of the area were not terribly rich, but certainly good enough, and by 1890 Shasta County ranked thirty-seventh in farm valuations among California's fifty-three counties. Cubic miles of toxic smoke thrown off by the new copper smelters of course tended to cause the Shasta settlers great distress. The stage was set for a most interesting quarrel.[2]

Extensive smelter-smoke damage to wild and cultivated vegetation on surrounding public and private lands brought on a tangled sequence of legal and political actions, a three-cornered struggle involving the smelting companies, local farmers, and the federal government. The conflict was bitterly agitated and heavily litigated. Ultimately the courts favored the smelters, reasoning that any injuries to the land and its owners were outweighed by the economic and social harm that would result from a stop-work injunction on some of the state's biggest industrial concerns. "The smelting industry is far too important to be sacrificed," the *San Francisco Chronicle* editorialized. "The smelters must stay, even if they do some damage." Heavy smelting of sulfurous ores continued in the Shasta district until world copper prices collapsed after the 1918 armistice.[3]

The environmental consequences, short term and long, were calamitous. At least one thousand square miles of farm, forest, and watershed land were adversely affected by smoke and fumes during the years when copper smelting was in full swing. Twenty years of airborne poisons followed by twenty years of fire and rain completely devastated over two hundred square miles—forty times the territory seared by the Hiroshima A-bomb. Millions of dollars of public money were

---

[2] Cronise, *The Natural Wealth of California*, 216–20; Lapham and Holmes, *Soil Survey of the Redding Area, California*, 5–13; Eleventh U.S. Census, 1890: Agriculture, 200.
[3] *San Francisco Chronicle*, September 19, 1906.

spent in a mostly ineffective effort to check massive soil erosion and restore a healthy plant cover in the barren area.
Problems with erosion and revegetation persist to this day.
This dramatic story has slumbered in the files for almost a
century; its scattered fragments have yet to be pieced together into a comprehensive account.

There has been no scholarship on the California smelter
area and its history, hence I have no one else's evidence to re-
visit and no earlier conclusions to review. My attention was
directed to the topic not by any reading but by my chance
discovery of some arresting images in a neglected collection
of old photographs. I sensed a story worth telling, saw that
the facts would have to be excavated entirely from archival
and other primary sources, and so began digging. I felt chal-
lenged by a detective mystery of a peculiar kind—the "murder of a landscape," to swipe a phrase from Edwin Way Teale.
The what and when of the killing were fairly apparent. The
questions that needed delving into were who, how, and why.
So I was drawn into a small adventure in industrial and political history, local, regional, and national.

All in all I was lucky in the quantity and quality of the
material I managed to unearth. Intact files of newspapers and
industry journals were tracked down in various libraries and
read from end to end. Thousands of pages of federal court
documents and the voluminous correspondence of federal
executive departments were well preserved in the National
Archives and its regional branches. Material surviving in the
California State Archives and in Shasta County repositories
was comparatively scant, but the bits recovered were god-
sends in certain key places. Archives of the University of
California and business records of the United States Smelting, Refining, and Mining Company unfortunately rendered
me nothing, but I think that I have been able to research my
way around these shortfalls and finish with a presentable
analysis. It remains to preview briefly the chapters that fol-

low, establish some general context, and give the reader some indication of the author's point of view and tone of voice.

Despite rural California's long heritage of direct action and vigilantism, the California smoke war was fought out primarily in the courts and was articulated entirely in the language of law. The farmers of Shasta County based their case on the time-honored law of nuisance, while the smelters based theirs on recent modifications thereof. Legal textbooks relate that twentieth-century environmental regulation arose partly from the traditional law of nuisance and partly from the nineteenth-century stagnation and decline of that tradition. Anglo-American common law and case law had immemorially favored settled and established uses of property over activities novel and disruptive to a neighborhood. The air and water that flowed cleanly and naturally over any proprietor's land were deemed inviolable as the land itself, and any activity that tended to spoil the setting was regarded as a nuisance, per se offensive and unlawful. But as the Industrial Revolution made headway and the influence of absentee investment stretched out, the old attitude was superseded by a new theory that preached the "balancing" of competing economic interests. Increasingly, any enterprise that supplied more wages to the public and more revenue to the realm was favored over more staid considerations of local and personal rights. The injunction, a court's sternest answer to insults to individual property, was witnessed much less frequently, and even awards for damages, the consolation prize in these cases, were less forthcoming. Blackstone no doubt would have been flabbergasted. This swing of legal doctrine, still in progress when the twentieth century opened, is central to this story.[4]

A contemporary political scientist wrote a book elucidating

---

[4] Percival, Miller, Schroeder, and Leape, *Environmental Regulation*, 73–88; Brenner, "Nuisance Law and the Industrial Revolution," 403–33. See also Coase, "The Problem of Social Cost," 19–28. Compare Kelley, *Battling the Inland Sea*, 218; Rice, Bullough, and Orsi, *The Elusive Eden*, 292.

something probably every Tammany operative already took for granted: under the hammer of interest group pressure "the finest legal logic is but a trivial fly-by-night, and the very essence of unreliability." Chapter 1 takes a look at interest group pressure at the grass roots, as the Mountain Copper Company of Great Britain established itself in Shasta County and immediately overrode all other interests. Local farmers sued the smelter repeatedly in local court but were beaten at every turn. The supporting cast here was wide and the potential for satire rather rich. In the pro-smelter cheering of Shasta County's sergeants of commerce—the owners of its banks and stores, the keepers of its bed houses and saloons, the editors of its daily papers—we witness in full sail two qualities Thorstein Veblen saw as key to the ethos of the contemporary American country town, "collusive cupidity" and "salesmanlike pusillanimity." In the shabby opportunism of University of California faculty and administrators, we see in flower similar qualities Veblen laughed at in the contemporary American university. We get the distinct feeling that "domestic colonialism," the "plundered province thesis," and other such abstractions of later commentators would have sounded extremely thin and far-fetched to all these provincial go-getters. So a note of archness and irony unavoidably creeps into the narrative, but I have tried to be physician-like, reporting the facts of the matter matter-of-factly, as symptoms of a broad and genuine consensus however comic or corrupt the manifestation. Like it or not, we are driven to the conclusion that majority opinion in the region at the time sincerely hankered for industrial investment at any cost and saw any opposition to it as just what one regional paper called it, "an attack on the most vital interests of the commonwealth."[5]

---

[5] Bentley, *The Process of Government*, 397; Veblen, *Absentee Ownership and Business Enterprise in Recent Times*, 156, 159; Brechin, *Imperial San Francisco*, 303–304; Robbins, "The 'Plundered Province' Thesis," 77–97; *San Francisco Call*, January 23, 1899.

Woodrow Wilson observed around this time that the history of a nation is no more than the history of its villages writ large. Chapter 2 concentrates on the U.S. government's case against Mountain Copper, through its dawdling pursuit in federal district and appellate courts in 1903–1906 and finally to its waffling compromise before the U.S. Supreme Court in 1908. We might have expected a firmer and more conservative stance from the upper floors of the nation's judiciary, especially when the nation's own property was at stake, but here again the legal system reflected the proindustry zeitgeist. Historians of American jurisprudence have noted the willingness of state and federal courts during this period to refashion long-standing doctrines to suit emerging capitalist demands. Across all departments of tort and property law—the law of nuisance being no exception—established rights of complainants were progressively trimmed and chiseled to accommodate the interests of industrial growth and capital accumulation. "We were a people going places in a hurry," Willard Hurst, a legal scholar, reflected in the 1950s. "We did not devote the prime energies of our legal growth to those who sought the law's shelter simply for what they had; our enthusiasm ran rather to those who wanted the law's help positively to bring things about." Hurst rather softly characterized this trend as a "release of energy" that favored active "ventures" over mere "holdings"—"dynamic rather than static property, property in motion and at risk rather than property secure and at rest." Later scholars interpreted the trend in a more critical light. Morton Horwitz, writing in the 1970s, saw "a deep tendency to favor the powerful" that amounted to a major subsidization of rising capitalist power. Refusal of injunctions and reduction or elimination of damage judgments constituted, he believed, a substantial "new source of forced investment," as less important property owners whose interests were impaired without compensation "in effect were compelled to underwrite a portion of economic growth." And in the latter class, Uncle Sam himself apparently was no exception.[6]

And if the national government was helpless against such an undertow, Shasta County farmers and ranchers were pretty clearly doomed when they remounted their attack on the copper industry in 1909, this time not as individual complainants but as members of a countywide league. Chapters 3 and 4 carry this phase of the story through its fizzling conclusion in 1915. Here the struggle was not against the original nemesis but against two new smelters established a little farther up the Sacramento canyon. Both operations were absentee-owned; both were creatures of the period of aggressive acquisition and overinvestment that historians of American business would dub the "Era of Corporate Prosperity." The Rockefellers did not want to leave the blossoming copper prospects of California entirely to the Rothschilds, while the Guggenheims did not want to risk being outflanked by the Rockefellers. One of the new smelters proved commercially unviable in the slump of 1907–1911, while the other shouldered through the crisis. The one conveniently blamed its demise on persecution by farmers, while the other went on to prosper, and snooked the farmers right along. Concerning the farmers' plight, the overriding attitude of the court system and of California society at large remained serenely indifferent. The farmers strenuously invoked the public good but never were able to recruit much of the public to their cause. The Southern Pacific Railroad Company, their strongest potential ally next to the federal government, showed some sympathy but considered its position as the region's major freight handler and ultimately stood back from

---

[6] Hurst, *Law and the Conditions of Freedom in the Nineteenth-Century United States*, 9–10, 24; Horwitz, *The Transformation of American Law*, 70, 102. See also Scheiber, "Property Law, Expropriation, and Resource Allocation by Government," 232–51; Pisani, "Enterprise and Equity," 15–37.

the fray, deciding that its interests lay on the side that
would "produce the greater traffic." The dollars-and-cents
sensibility of the Southern Pacific management was the
rule, not the exception. Bourgeois conservation groups like
the Sierra Club and the California Water and Forest Association, and even agrarian groups like the California State
Grange, also maintained an attitude of neutrality—as a
matter of fact, rank indifference. The bolder stripe of anti-
corporation sentiment in California progressivism already
had started to fade by this time, and the legislative and executive branches of the state government rendered only
token assistance.[7]

Chapter 5 wraps up the story of the federal government's
halfhearted effort to uphold the integrity of national property
against the menace of smelter fumes. In 1913 the government ended up dropping its bid for an injunction against the
Mammoth and Balaklala smelters and settled its claim for injuries to the public domain for less than forty cents an acre.
This phase of the story uncovers no real surprises. Gabriel
Kolko has shown how it was increasing domination of government by big business, not vice versa, that was the salient
tendency in federal politics throughout this, the so-called
Progressive Era. "One must discard completely the struggle
against corporations as the setting in which to understand
conservation history," declares Samuel Hays, another leading
scholar of this period. The California smoke war was brought
to an end at long last not by any political intervention but by
contraction of the global copper market and exhaustion of
the Shasta ores. By way of denouement, chapter 5 ends with
a discussion of the costly reclamation campaign waged at
public expense in the eroded, mountainous parts of the

---

[7] Hacker, Modley, and Taylor, *The United States: A Graphic History*, 199; Marcosson,
Metal Magic, 70–83; Baruch, *Baruch: My Own Story*, 196–99; Orsi, *Sunset Limited, 1850–
1930*, 585n62; Mowry, *The California Progressives*, 221, 289–90.

Shasta smoke zone thirty years after the blast furnaces went cold. A staggering inventory of what British planners call "derelict land" belied the incredibly weak arithmetic of the U.S. government officials who settled accounts with the copper companies in 1908 and 1913. In fact the rehabilitation of this, the nation's largest man-made desert, was a considerably bigger and tougher undertaking than the creation of its largest man-made forest, half a continent away in the Sand Hills of western Nebraska.[8]

All along we have to admire the sharp game played by the industry, yet much of the smelters' apparent gamesmanship was no more than good fortune. They clearly had the weight of public opinion and the trajectory of American legal doctrine going for them. In addition, the most critical junctures in the California smoke litigation happened to come to a head during or not long after the "Rich Man's Panic" of 1903–1904, the "Roosevelt Panic" of 1907–1908, and the "War Depression" of 1913–1914, when copper prices sagged, smelter output was cut back, field evidence of smoke damage was less striking than usual, and judges and other officials were especially reluctant to place additional burdens on an apparently shaky domestic industry. The smelters also benefited fortuitously from the shortcomings of contemporary science. Although the bad effects of sulfur dioxide on plants and people had been recognized for at least a century, exact details of the pathology of the gas were still far from resolved, so the law's narrow rules of evidence and liability could be skirted almost indefinitely given a friendly expert witness or two—always on tap given the industry's readiness to pay. And not the least of the industry's advantages was the general unimportance of the land in controversy. Statistics from the U.S. census of agriculture show that Shasta County's commercial orchard and vine-

---

[8] Kolko, *The Triumph of Conservatism*; Hays, *Conservation and the Gospel of Efficiency*, 2; Barr, *Derelict Britain*; Pool, "Forty Years on the Nebraska National Forest," 139–59.

yard acreage declined 40 percent during the copper-smelting
era (1900–1920), obviously a grievous setback to the individuals and families concerned. But overall California's booming
horticulture industry was barely nicked: at its peak the county
had accounted for not much more than 1 percent of the state's
total tree and vine inventory. The federal government had a
similar public relations problem fighting for a remote and un-
remarkable section of foothill woodland, the commercial and
aesthetic value of which was easily written off in the minds of
most constituents.[9]

The small wrinkles of big matters make worthwhile study
and so do the big wrinkles of small matters. I think this con-
tribution to the political, industrial, and environmental history of California should pass by one standard or the other,
if not by both. But it is submitted as nothing more than the
inside story of one remarkable situation and how it came to
be and how it ended up, with the focus always on local land
and life. It does not aspire to be a treatise on the evolution
of American civil law, or a manual on industrial air pollution, or a dissertation on the history of mining and metallurgical technology, or a meditation on globalization and
social conflict. It is not framed as "western history," or as
"new western history," either. I culled the extensive literature of those and other fields only to supply a few useful
guideposts, and I only hope my selection was adequate and
fair and nowhere misleading. I have tried to lay out the story
line in as plain and compact a manner as the diffuse and
complicated character of the source material admits, but
what body and drama the chronicle has is inherent in the
material and not the result of any art of mine.

---

[9] Herfindahl, *Copper Costs and Prices, 1870–1957*, 80–91; Flamant and Singer-Kárel,
Modern Economic Crises, 42–51; Grant-Francis, *The Smelting of Copper in the Swansea Dis-
trict*, 137, 151–60; Weldon, "Smelter Fumes Injury to Vegetation," 240–49; Wirth, *Smelter
Smoke in North America*, 45–79; U.S. Bureau of the Census, Thirteenth U.S. Census, 1910:
Agriculture, 160, 164.

CHAPTER ONE

"The interest of this community"

"I understand they have made it their boast, that they can do as they please here in this Country and no one would dare to interfere with them. I trust for the good name of our Government and for the interest of this community, that they will speedily be brought to justice and receive a lesson they will long remember." That was the frank conclusion of Henry Cullom's confidential report to Binger Hermann, commissioner of the U.S. General Land Office, in March 1898. Special Agent Cullom had been assigned to investigate a peculiar trespass case in northern California's Shasta County. A string of complaints from people in the region had informed the U.S. Department of the Interior that the Mountain Copper Company, a British syndicate working the Iron Mountain copper mine, north of Redding, not only was supplying its operation with huge volumes of lumber and fuel wood plundered from nearby public lands, but the poisonous fumes and gases given off in the processing of its ores were killing all the timber and grass within a radius of at least ten miles.

Cullom came to Redding in February 1898 and spent over two weeks on his investigation. He experienced unusual difficulty getting witnesses who were willing to supply information. "Nearly every one I have approached on the subject would say yes, the mining company and others are cutting a great deal of timber and wood from Government land and the sulphur and arsenic are killing all the trees and vegetation for miles around, but I don't care to antagonize this Company by being a witness against them." After persistent prying he managed to secure a number of affidavits establishing the fact that "promiscuous timber stealing" was indeed rampant in the neighborhood, and nearly all of it was carried on at the behest and behoof of the London corporation. He uncovered a ring of local contractors who had discovered the trick of having their workers file batches of free mining claims on government land, after which they quickly stripped the land of all saw timber and cordwood, then cleanly abandoned their bogus filings. One rogue employing this technique already had gotten away with over seven thousand cords, delivered to the Mountain Copper Company for $2.50 a cord.

Cullom rented a horse and personally inspected several sections on the far side of Iron Mountain where depredations were in progress. On some of these tracts the timber—"very valuable timber, large sugar and yellow pine"—already had been cut down and removed; other tracts as yet uncut were blanketed with recent "mining claims" that had been cunningly staked out to enclose all the good standing pine, even though there were no surface indications of mineral deposits and no evidence of bona fide efforts to find any. Cullom served cease-and-desist warnings on those culprits he was able to identify and forwarded their names to Washington for further action. Thus far the situation was no different from scores of others the General Land Office had to deal with every year in the western states.

An unprecedented and indeed much more alarming feature of this case was the far-reaching effect on surrounding vegetation of the smoke and fumes discharged by the com-

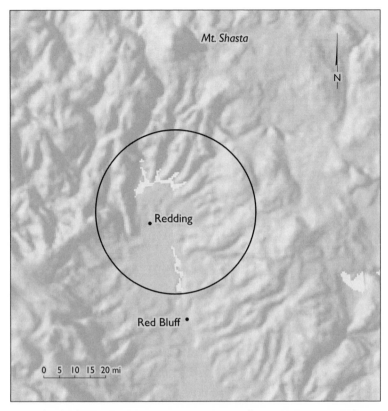

Shaded relief map encompassing approximately 10,000 square miles at the northern end of the Sacramento Valley, California. Centered on the city of Redding, lat. 40° 36" N, long. 122° 25" W, elev. 555 feet. Circle indicates the area visibly impacted by smelter smoke, as established by numerous affidavits and reports, 1903–14. Scale 1:1,250,000.

pany's smelter. "There is not grass enough growing on any thousand acres of land within two miles of these copper ore roasters to pasture one cow," Cullom declared. "I have since my arrival here visited all sides north, south, east, and west of the Mountain Copper Company's works and I find that nearly all the timber and brush and vegetation of every description of whatsoever nature is either entirely dead or dying." Unless something was done immediately, Cullom predicted, "in two years from now everything within ten miles of the roasting pits of the copper mining company in the nature of timber, fruit trees, shrubbery, bushes, grass, and all else will be a thing of the past, and I base my opinion upon what has been the effect in this vicinity in the last two or three years."[1]

A succession of local entrepreneurs had worked Iron Mountain with indifferent success for some twenty years before the complex ore formation drew notice from scouts for a group of London capitalists associated with the famous Rio Tinto mines of Spain. In 1895 those canny investors bought the property for $300,000, then proceeded to expose a deep mass of pyrite and chalcopyrite whose copper, silver, and gold contents were conservatively appraised at $50 million. The Mountain Copper Company was quickly organized, and capital was liberally invested in mining facilities, a narrow gauge railroad, and a well-equipped smelting plant in Spring Creek canyon about six miles northwest of Redding. Next to the new smelter they laid out a new town, naming the place after Lord William Keswick, the gentleman who chaired the company's board of directors. The first blast furnace was hissing by the spring of 1896, two more were in commission by fall, and by year's end the operation was running smoothly and profitably. In 1897 the Keswick plant extracted more than 165,000 tons of ore, yielding $2.8 million in copper and $1.7 million in silver and gold. The fledgling company reported net profits of over $2.3 million, making for a dividend of 34 percent on its declared capitalization of $7 million. Almost

---

[1] Cullom to commissioner of General Land Office, March 8, 1898, in GLO 30.

overnight, it had become the biggest mining enterprise in California.[2]

The company's ore was rich in metallic values but richer still in a waste element highly noxious to both man and vegetation. Intimately combined with the copper, silver, and gold in Iron Mountain chalcopyrite was an exceptionally generous measure of Hell's own brimstone. Sulfur in fact constituted 40–45 percent of the typical ore sample. Under the smelting methods then in vogue, the excess sulfur had to be eliminated before the ore was charged into the blast furnaces. This was accomplished most cheaply and expeditiously by calcining or "roasting" the green ore in enormous outdoor heaps. It was this phase of the operation that excited the greatest indignation and brought on the clash with Uncle Sam. The lower end of Spring Creek basin was covered with a network of switches and sidetracks radiating from the big bunkers where raw ore from the mine was sorted and stored. Temporary trestles, arching long and low, were built in the open spaces. Under the trestles huge beds of cordwood were laid down, wide as a city street and hundreds of feet long. Ore was trammed from the bunkers in dump cars, pulled up the trestles, and piled and spread on the cordwood beds to a height of eight feet or so. Rough plank chimneys stuffed with kindling were installed at close intervals along the length of the ore heaps. When a heap was finished and ready for firing, the trestle was dismantled, then coal oil was poured down the chimneys and ignited. The long mass then was left to flare, flicker, and smolder for several months. After some two-thirds of the sulfur had been driven off, the heap was opened up with a steam shovel and the roasted ore was carried off to the blast furnaces.[3]

[2] Aubury, *The Copper Resources of California*, 43–44, 70–76; *Redding Free Press*, April 2, 1898; Kett, "Fifty Years of Operation by the Mountain Copper Company, Ltd., in Shasta County, California," 108–21.

[3] Neilson, "Roasting Copper Ore at Keswick, California," 457–58.

By 1898 the Keswick blast furnaces were putting through
more than six hundred tons a day, and to keep them fed with
a steady supply of roasted ore it was necessary to keep a great
many of those poisonous bonfires burning. "With its nine great
smokestacks and its acres of roasting fields it looks in the busy
season like a great burning town," said one fascinated reporter.
The toll on the local environment was appalling. As many as
thirty thousand cords of fuel wood were being fetched every
year from the surrounding hills, most of it cut illegally. Hundreds of thousands of tons of smoking ore were spread out on
the flats and hillsides along Spring Creek. Sulfur dioxide and
other choking fumes rolled off the serried roast piles in yellow-
white clouds, flowing down the gulches and eddying over the
hills, hanging over the area like a foul fog when the weather
was still. The environs of Keswick turned into a virtual
Gehenna as the smoke killed off every tree, every blade of
grass, every hardy weed. The bright green hair and whiskers
and weirdly tinted skins of the miserable roast-yard stiffs were
minor compensations for the loss of all natural verdure, a San
Francisco visitor sardonically remarked.[4]

It did not take long for people living in the vicinity to develop an anxious interest in what was taking place. "Opinion is shaping itself to a decided degree," Shasta resident
Charles Paige told the *Sacramento Record-Union* in 1897.
The smoke's ill effects on human health and comfort had become apparent right away. The unnatural fumes were nause-
ating and suffocating, making the district "almost
uninhabitable" to many persons, Paige complained. The
lethal influence of sulfur dioxide on local plant life was even
more striking. The hills surrounding Keswick already were
covered with "masses of dead trees and blasted shrubbery."

---

[4] *Mining and Scientific Press* 76 (1898), 561; *San Francisco Call*, April 20, 1902; *Engineering and Mining Journal* 76 (1903), 365; *San Francisco Chronicle*, April 26, 1903; Kett,
"Fifty Years of Operation by Mountain Copper," 117–18.

Brush and forest fires, Paige accurately warned, "will quickly leave the hills bare of all signs of vegetation, and an expanse of baked soil and rocks, shimmering in the heat of summer, and washing into gullies and gorges with the winter rains." The destruction already was in evidence for miles, he assured; its ultimate extent could only be conjectured. Not only were unoccupied government lands threatened, but privately owned farms and orchards were being destroyed and innocent settlers were being smoked out of their very homes. Here, Paige protested, was the spectacle of an alien corporation allowed to invade a section of American territory, denuding the land and evicting its native-born occupants. "These things are of those that shake the faith of men in their own works, in their own government, and chill patriotism into indifference, or derision," he concluded bitterly. "An American citizen is, or is supposed to be, guaranteed certain constitutional rights, but when these are infringed he is (if poor) as helpless as an inverted mud-turtle on a marble slab."[5]

Sentiments like those festered sorely as the evidence of smoke and fumes damage accumulated. The General Land Office dispatched Special Agent Cullom to the area the following February. Cullom investigated the situation honestly and aggressively, and he recommended that the Mountain Copper Company be "prosecuted to the full extent of the law." General Land Office Commissioner Binger Hermann moved promptly enough on the matter. He decided that action on Cullom's finding of illegal timber cutting should await fuller investigation but the fumes problem warranted immediate attention. He asked that the Justice Department be directed to take steps to procure an order of injunction against the copper company. The government, he intoned,

---

[5] Paige, "A Complaint from Shasta," 5.

"cannot allow the life and growth of the timber upon the public lands to be injured or jeopardized to any degree by the smelting or ore roasting operations of the said company, which destroys more timber than is accomplished by the unlawful felling thereof for fuel and mining purposes." On June 16, 1898, the U.S. attorney in San Francisco filed a bill for injunction in federal district court, charging, in the starched language of the complaint, "that the sulphurous and arsenical fumes and smoke generated and produced by roasting and burning said copper and other ores have greatly injured and destroyed and still are so injuring and destroying vast quantities of said trees and timber and rendering valueless said lands on which the same are situated, to your orator's great and irreparable injury and damage."[6]

Disclosure of the government's action immediately hit the front pages of California's public prints, crowded but not concealed by the thrilling war news from Cuba and the Philippines. "Redding is worried," observed a San Francisco paper. "The people generally up there tolerate the fumes and the square miles of dead scrub pine very cheerfully because of the prosperity which attends the expenditure of so much money and the support of so large a population." The big money from Iron Mountain might have been rolling to London, but enough rubbed off at the source to put most local sentiment foursquare behind the Mountain Copper Company. Employing one thousand men at its mine and smelter, the company was disbursing over $60,000 a month in wages, virtually all of which funneled straight into the cash registers of Redding merchants—and to that circle especially the sour smoke and environmental ruin around the big smelter signaled not desolation but milk and honey. It kept the hotels overflow-

    [6] Commissioner of General Land Office to secretary of interior, March 30, 1898, in DOI 5154-1897; "Bill of Complaint," June 16, 1898, in NDC 12633.

ing and vitalized all branches of commerce. The possibility that an industry on which maybe half the city's business now depended might be shut down while the smoke issue wound its weary way through the meshes of the law was only a little less distressing than the prospect of a permanent closure should an adverse decision finally be reached. The fifteen hundred men directly and indirectly dependent on the company's operations would be thrown out of work, and merchants would abruptly lose their custom, along with the big sums of money expended by the company on its own account for supplies and services. Perhaps even more appalling, the outside capital needed to bring the area's copper resources to an even higher state of development was bound to shy away if it saw the operations of the pioneer investor being hampered by lawsuits.[7]

Redding newspapers automatically scurried to the corporation's defense. The *Searchlight* ridiculed federal intervention on behalf of "the magnificent manzanita and the stately chaparral" and denounced the government's suit as not just unnecessary but irresponsible—in fact, "the height of folly." A little doubtful damage to brush, scrub timber, and a few scattered homesteads was more than offset by the vast advantages which accrued to the community as a whole—or in the paper's own candid words, "the good that is done by the constant distribution of money far over-balances any bad." The timber, in any case, was not of milling quality, was useful only as fuel, and its value even as firewood was established only by the market furnished by the smelter. "It is simply brush," Lewis Wright, the company's resident manager, told the sympathetic *Free Press*, "and it is being cut and used for wood to supply the needs of the people of this district whose business here is due to and dependent upon the working of the smelter. If our

---

[7] *San Francisco Call*, June 28, 1898; *Redding Searchlight*, June 19, 1898.

works were not here this wood would be of no use to anyone."
And the notion that the smelter could ever eliminate or even
reduce its fumes was "all nonsense, nothing but a myth. How
can this great volume of smoke be condensed? What will become of it? And what will you do with it?" He went on to forecast a regular financial panic if the injunction were granted
and the plant shut down. It would withdraw at least $150,000
a month from local channels of trade; retail merchants would
be unable to collect outstanding bills, hence would be unable
to pay their wholesalers, "and as a result many business houses
will close."[8]

Mountain Copper did not have the advantage of owning
the region's newspapers outright, but self-interest, on a level
not much less abject, obviously was quite enough to bind
them to the smelter's side with rings of iron. The *Shasta
Courier* furnished the lone exception to the pattern of jour-
nalistic truckling to the imperial enterprise. The old Gold
Rush town of Shasta was just three miles from the new works,
with nothing but a few low hills standing between. "For more
than a year our people have submitted to a stench and desolation that they hoped would be temporary," exclaimed the
Courier, "and they now rejoice that the Government has
come to their rescue, and that the air we breathe shall no
longer bear poison and pollution on its wings." For weeks the
half-sheet kept up a running editorial fire on the "encroach-
ing, over-reaching, un-American" corporation, and called
for "the arm of beneficent Government" to extend itself
quickly. It poured special scorn on the "cringing county
press" and the "sordid gang" of local business leaders who
misrepresented the real state of things for the sake of the "few
paltry dollars" they derived from a foreign company that
looked on an American citizen "as it would upon a cheap-
labor Kaffir." The brazen corporation had sawed up lumber as

---

[8] *Redding Searchlight*, June 18, 24–25, 1898; *Redding Free Press*, July 2, 1898.

good as any produced anywhere from public land it now as-
serts was worthless, the *Courier* proclaimed. As for the social
benefits it claims to have conferred by establishing a new
town and creating a new center of trade and revenue: "It
costs this county more to take care of the criminals and
toughs of that outfit, and clustered around it, than all the rest
of the county put together."[9]

The company filed a demurrer to the government's complaint, and by raising various tedious questions of law prepared to stall action on the suit indefinitely. Through
out-of-court channels, meanwhile, it was urging an amicable adjustment and quiet settlement of the controversy. It
proposed to pay an agreed sum for the value of the destroyed
timber, "which shall operate as a complete settlement of the
Government's claim in that respect." It also proffered, "if
necessary," an agreed annual rental value for the lands affected. Of course a special agreement to lease the injured
public lands surrounding the smelter essentially would have
licensed and legalized the smoke nuisance in perpetuity. Still
taking a hard line, the General Land Office reported adversely on the proposal, pointing out that it was "neither
practicable in the absence of any statutory provision for the
rental of the public lands, nor could any indemnity be
thereby secured against further injury to which the public interests continue to be exposed." The U.S. attorney in San
Francisco meanwhile advised his superiors that "there is considerable complaint made by private owners, of damages
done to other lands owned by them in that vicinity."[10]

Considerable complaint indeed. A second epistle from

---

[9] *Shasta Weekly Courier*, June 25, July 9, 16, 23, 30, 1898. It is amusing to note that in
1887 the central California county of Fresno arranged to shift a generous slice of its territory encompassing the booming New Idria quicksilver mine onto neighboring San Benito
County, largely because of costly law-and-order problems around the New Idria works: see
Mylar, *Early Days at the Mission San Juan Bautista*, 36.

[10] H. S. Foote to attorney general, July 29, 1898, and acting commissioner of General
Land Office to secretary of interior, August 17, 1898, in DOI 5154-1897.

Charles Paige went so far as to imply that vigilante action
might be in store. The Keswick abomination was not something that was going to cure itself or fade away under a chaf-
fering policy, he told the *Sacramento Record-Union* in August
1898. "There is not at this time, and there has not been for
two years past, any reasonable excuse for further parley, technical investigation, recommendations, or other red-tape trifling. . . . There is no more virtue in temporizing with the
Keswick destruction than there would be in watching a
house burn up to see if the fire will go out." Fully a quarter of
a million acres of valuable public and private property were
being deforested, contaminated, and rendered uninhabitable,
Paige claimed. Valuable orchards, vineyards, and stock
ranches would soon be abandoned by their proprietors, while
the killing of the wild growth on the mountainsides would
certainly bring on fire, flood, and other ruinous results. If the
government was going to coddle the destructive activities of
the Mountain Copper Company, he declared, "it is a silly
parody to molest minor and insignificant vandals and
depredators. If a hundred homes may be devastated with im-
punity so openly, why should there be any restrictions upon
the robbery of mere stage coaches or banks?" By its inaction,
Paige cried, the government was sacrificing not just the hard-
won property but the basic constitutional rights of its citizens to a cynical and mercenary, and withal a foreign-owned,
corporation.[11]

Brush fires crackled over wide portions of the smoke zone
that month, drawing especially furious comment from the
Shasta Courier:

> An area of miles—an area that is constantly extending—is
> being slowly but surely smoked and dried into what will be, or what
> now are, furnaces of fiery heat. For days past the smoke and intense

---

[11] Paige, "Devastation at Keswick," 2.

heat of the burning fume-blasted forests about Redding and Shasta have been fatal to not only vegetable but to human life. . . . Even God's own free and bright sunshine is shut out by this lurid, smoking hell of destruction and death, and the orb of day comes and goes, not in the glory of sunrise, or evening sunset splendor—it rises and sinks as dull and copper-colored as the gall of the Mountain Copper Company management, in heavens that were blue and free and unpolluted until a soulless foreign corporation took possession of this portion of the State of California, that was once supposed to be under the laws and protection of the Flag of the United States of America.[12]

The outcry in northern California attracted the notice of the *San Francisco Call,* which sent correspondent J. F. Rose-Soley upcountry to review the situation. By now the Keswick plant employed over a thousand men; with dependents and hangers-on the smelter town numbered well over two thousand souls. A motley parade of tramps and roustabouts was perpetually coming and going, for nobody, Jack or Dago, stayed at the loathsome work any longer than he had to. The creation and support of this industrial community was one of the achievements the company proudly pointed out to those who sought to restrain its operations. Rose-Soley found something other than the boasted thrift and prosperity. "Keswick today bears awful testimony to the triumph of ruthless Capital over innocent Nature," he wrote. "I do not know whether Keswick was ever a pretty place, or whether it was even a place at all before the smelting works came there, but today it certainly looks as if the Deity had learned to ignore its existence." He sketched a picture of moral desolation that matched the morbid environment:

Imagine the hideous newness of a mining camp combined with the noisy tinkling vice of the Barbary Coast. Bare unpainted wooden houses and shanties are scattered all over the barren hill-

---

[12] *Shasta Weekly Courier,* August 6, 1898.

Environs of Keswick by the summer of 1903. The picture speaks for itself. Photograph by J. K. Haywood. Taken from his *Injury to Vegetation by Smelter Fumes*, U.S. Bureau of Chemistry Bulletin 89 (Washington, D.C., 1905).

side without any apparent arrangement, for as yet there are more vacant allotments than dwellings in the township. The place centers upon a high wooden fence, which marks the boundary of the smelting works. Upon the gate is announced, with true British conservatism, the fact that the ground within is private property and that no trespassers will be permitted. Still, despite the threatening inscription, the gate stands wide open and anybody who chooses may walk in and out.

Close to the entrance is a long line of wooden shanties, each of which is a gin mill of the lowest description. Though it is not yet high noon, beery, unshaved men lounge about the sidewalk and stagger in and out of the dens, holding, after the manner of drunken men, loud and aimless discussions upon nothing in particular. The works run day and night, consequently there are always a number of men off duty, and the saloons are never empty. Occasionally, to vary the monotony of everlasting beer, there is a free fight, and the one doctor, who lives in the only decent hotel the place possesses, just over the way, is called upon to patch a broken head, or to sew up an ugly jagged wound caused by a bottle. Shooting cases are rare. The bottle or the knife is the favorite weapon. The pop, pop, pop of a shooting gallery indicates the only form of innocent recreation available, while farther down the hill, where the company's fence rises to double its usual height, is a large wooden building in which the scarlet woman holds sway. The midday sun shines with overpowering heat on the unsheltered place. There is not a flower or a green thing to be seen; even the trees on the hillside hang their withered brown tassels in despair. No form of vegetation can grow in such an accursed spot. Only man, impelled by need or greed, strives to drag on a miserable existence there.

Rose-Soley did not have to be a professional chemist to put his finger on the source of the problem. "SO_2—It is only a simple little chemical formula, looking quite innocent and harmless in print; yet, when let loose by man's agency upon an unsuspecting vegetable world it means terrible mischief."

Though the air is clear, there is a noticeable smell of sulphur everywhere, just as if someone had struck a match under your nose. The residents don't notice it. "This is nothing," said a dried-up looking man as he tilted his chair back on the veranda. "It's a dry day. Wait till we get some wet weather and then you will see the fumes settle down on the town like a pall, and almost choke the life out of you."

I declined the invitation, for even on a clear hot day there was quite as much sulphur about as was pleasant. The hill slopes sharply down from the town into a deep canyon, and here, nestling round the banks of what was once a clear mountain stream, rise huge sheds and tall iron chimneys. The stream has long since disappeared. Viscid pools of ugly yellow and gray slime have taken its place, but it is worth noticing that the gully drains into the Sacramento. When the rainy season sets in, and a flood of water rushes down the canyon, all this refuse must be washed down into the river, polluting the beautiful stream and destroying the fish for many miles.

Wildfires were still burning in several places, and it was anyone's guess how far the desolation of the surrounding country would proceed this year and how much would be left to next summer's flames. Except for the transient roughnecks employed at the works and the storekeepers who catered to them, people in the vicinity intensely resented the state of affairs, but conflicting interests, real or fancied, kept them from getting too vocal. Even people in the village of Shasta had come to understand the better part of valor:

> Naturally the residents of this old established mining town, which is only some three miles from the smelter, are extremely indignant, though, for reasons which can be readily understood, they are very cautious in giving expression to their indignation. They will talk freely enough in confidence, but they invariably extort a promise that their name shall not appear in print. A good many people from the works live in Shasta; there are local and business interests to be considered, and no one dares to proclaim himself the enemy of such a great corporation. "I will give Shasta just ten years to become as barren as Keswick," said one resident, "that is, if a bush fire does not destroy it before." "There is more sickness in the town than was ever known before," says another. "People get carried off by some mysterious complaint, and we can only attribute it to the fumes."

Of course the good citizens of the county seat had learned to muffle their indignation early on. "Redding is a strictly commercial place; its citizens derive profit in many ways from the smelter and the men who work it. So they don't like to say too much, but they admit that on a wet day, if the wind happens to be in the right direction, the shrubs and flowers in their gardens shrivel up under the poisonous fumes. The sulphur even attacks the paint on their houses."

Taking away the copper, silver, and gold of the ore for the enrichment of its shareholders in England, the Mountain Copper Company graciously left the toxic fumes and residues to the people of California. "The bargain," Rose-Soley wryly observed, "is rather too one-sided to be fair." The region rejoiced in a fine climate and an abundance of good soil, but the settlers' vision of a countryside covered with verdant orchards was dying away under the blight of smelter fumes. The rational development of the district was being retarded and discouraged, and this perhaps was the most shameful aspect of the situation. "It is no wonder that the residents despair; unless the evil is checked there is nothing before the country but barren desolation, overhung by a cloud of sulphurous smoke." Rose-Soley noted that the federal government recently had taken steps to restrict the smelter, but it was evident that the corporation was going to put up a strong fight. The progress of the case promised to be painfully slow and its final outcome was doubtful. That no relief would be had except under absolute compulsion was certain.[13]

On the sidewalks of Keswick and Redding, indignation over Rose-Soley's write-up was "thicker than any smoke," according to the *Free Press*. "If the special correspondent had appeared on the streets he would have been forcibly dealt with. He had better keep at a safe distance from now until the end of the world." The towns loved the smelter, made no apologies, and would brook no liars, the paper roared. "Damage to the forests!" it snorted. "Over a space of four square miles the 'forest' has been damaged—yes, killed. But what is death to scrub pine, manzanita, chaparral, and greasewood? . . . The smoke has not yet anywhere destroyed a single forest tree that would be recognized at a sawmill." As for allegations that the smoke was inimical to human health—

[13] Rose-Soley, "Sulphurous Fumes Devastate Shasta County," 5.

why, everybody knew the sickness prevailing in the district was nothing more than a little common malaria.[14]

It certainly was not trying to drum up prejudice against any new enterprise, but neither could it turn a deaf ear to the complaints of the despoiled, the *San Francisco Call* explained in an editorial a few days later. There was, it went on to comment, nothing new in the plea that the destruction wrought by industries producing great wealth was both morally and economically justified. It might be true as some claimed that the hills around Keswick were not fit for agriculture and the commercial value of the timber growing on them was nil. But the point lost all merit as a moral or economic argument when it was considered that the despised brush and scrub was an important factor in preserving the watershed of the Sacramento River and thus the fertility and well-being of the whole Sacramento Valley, "from Redding to Rio Vista." Mining after all was a self-limiting enterprise that would be forgotten when the ores petered out, but the productivity of forest and farm land was everlasting if properly protected, "as permanent as the soil itself." Injuries of the kind inflicted by the Mountain Copper Company had to be restrained for the sake of "the far-reaching future of this State, the fertility of its soil and its capacity to sustain a dense population," which directly depended on the conservation of its mountain and foothill woodlands. Floods, soil erosion, and climate change would be the sure penalties otherwise. "In no respect are these things speculative or theoretical. They are demonstrated over and over again in older countries and the experience of more than two thousand years."[15]

After the initial flurry of attention little more was heard of the government's suit, which was allowed to drift on the dis-

---

[14] *Redding Free Press*, August 27, 1898.
[15] *San Francisco Call*, September 2, 1898.

trict court's docket from one session to the next. The U.S. attorney failed to press for a preliminary injunction, perhaps fondly hoping that by merely holding a lawsuit over the company's head it could be induced to modify its operations without a struggle. It was known that Mountain Copper for its part much preferred a cash settlement of the U.S. government's claim to any forced abridgment of its smelting methods, and was making offers to that effect. There were hopes that one way or another the claim would be quietly adjusted and the whole issue discreetly dropped. Certainly, the interests that created Keswick had ridden out worse challenges before. The same Rothschild capital that backed Mountain Copper stood behind the Rio Tinto Company, which was smelting copper sulfide ores on an even greater scale at Huelva in southern Spain. In 1888, local outrage over the company's open-air roast piles had climaxed in vicious riots that left a hundred protesters dead. The Rio Tinto operation was roundly denounced in the Spanish parliament and the specter of nationalization was raised. The company managed to detoxify the political atmosphere with a judicious distribution of indemnities to landowners and bribes to legislators and labor bosses, and it was able to persist in its ore-roasting practices at Huelva for another twenty years.[16]

Here in America's "Wild West," affairs were set to move on a much more sedate and sluggish track. Mountain Copper filed its formal answer to the U.S. government's complaint on May 2, 1899. It insisted that the United States had not been injured substantially because the land was "absolutely worthless" to begin with—it was, in fact, nothing but "waste, mountainous, and desert land," the soil "thin and barren," the vegetation no more than "a thin growth of trees and bushes" whose value "never was greater than $1 an acre." In

[16] Avery, *Not on Queen Victoria's Birthday*, 196–98, 301.

this so-styled wasteland the company had built up a "great industry," and it was conducting this industry in the only manner that was commercially feasible. If restrained by
injunction from roasting its ores it would be prevented from
working its mines at all, and its entire investment of seven
million dollars would be laid up and rendered useless. Hundreds of workingmen, the nation's own citizens, would be
rooted up and scattered to the four winds. "The defendant,"
the company told the court, "has offered and still offers to
pay to the complainant in cash the full amount of all injury
and damage which it has caused." This offer to compromise
had the effect of staving off a temporary restraining order and
tied up proceedings in the case for several years.[17]

Next month the company submitted a fresh proposition
of settlement. From the Southern Pacific Railroad Company
it had purchased 4,750 acres in ten alternate sections in Kern
County, over four hundred miles south of the scene of controversy. These tracts were situated as in-holdings in the
Sierra Forest Reserve, created by executive order six years
before. The copper company proposed to deed this land over
to the government in exchange for the 4,590 acres of Shasta
County land described in the latter's bill of complaint, under
terms of an 1897 statute that allowed holders of private property in the new forest reserves to trade their land to the government for an equivalent acreage of vacant, nonmineral
land elsewhere in the public domain. Obviously the company had decided it was easier to remove the government's
grounds for complaint by buying up all the remaining public
land in the smoke zone than it was to remove the cause of
complaint by abridging its operations or installing appliances
to purify the noxious fumes. The General Land Office agreed
to take the offer under consideration, though it was unsure

[17] "Answer of Mountain Copper Company," May 2, 1899, in NDC 12633.

how such an exchange could affect a claim for damages done prior to any rights that might accrue to the company under the deal.[18]

There was certainly nothing in Mountain Copper's production reports to suggest any voluntary curtailment of operations while the injunction suit and land-exchange application were pending. The smelter worked up over six hundred thousand tons of Iron Mountain ore over the next two years, delighting its London shareholders with over $5 million in net earnings. This was the springtide of the Age of Electricity—the industrial world was being wired for light and power, and demand for the red metal was roaring. It is significant to note that the gross value of Keswick copper in 1900 (almost $5 million) was still a nose ahead of the gross reported by southern California's booming petroleum industry (a little over $4 million). In 1900 the company undertook a major remodeling and enlargement of its smelter. The infamous system of outdoor roast piles was given up, and a battery of twelve big mechanical turret roasters was installed for calcining the green ore. Two new blast furnaces were added to the original complement of three, raising the smelting capacity of the plant from 750 tons a day to 1,000 tons a day. In addition, three big converter stands were installed that spring. These were Bessemer-like units in which the matte or "black copper" from the blast furnaces, formerly shipped back to New Jersey for this next-to-last stage of treatment, was remelted and blown so as to oxidize most of the remaining sulfur and iron, leaving a fairly pure "blister copper" ready for electrolytic refining. All the new furnaces were fitted with hoods and connected by long flues to a set of tall chimneys. The company subsequently tried to claim a great

---

[18] Commissioner of General Land Office to secretary of interior, January 26, 1901, in DOI 5154-1897. See also Ise, *The United States Forest Policy*, 176–80.

amelioration of smoke conditions, but it is obvious that the net effect of these improvements was really a huge increase in the amount of sulfur dioxide delivered into the local atmosphere.[19]

The percentage yield of copper was falling off rather markedly as the richer levels of the Iron Mountain ore body were exhausted, but the decline in that regard was more than offset by the expanded plant capacity. Keswick enjoyed another banner year in 1901, turning out 31 million pounds of copper making its owners a clear profit of $1.8 million. The *San Francisco Post* marveled that the annual product of this five-year-old enterprise already showed a dollar-value half as great as the combined output of all the state's fabled gold mines. But a growing faction of farmers and ranchers in the neighborhood saw nothing to cheer in the smelter's past and present, and they were even less happy about its future prospects. Shasta County orchard growers were looking at a very disappointing fruit set in the spring of 1901, and while some attributed it to an untimely spell of cold weather, many more were inclined to fix blame on the smoke drifting down from Keswick. In March a two-day farmers' institute convened at Anderson under University of California auspices drew attendance from all over the county. The visiting professors offered presentations on the usual workaday topics, but unscheduled discussions quickly made it clear that the smoke problem was uppermost in the farmers' minds. A resolution forwarded to the university's board of regents explained that thousands of acres of actual and potential horticultural land were threatened with irreparable ruin by the "vast quantities of sulphurous smoke which settles over this district," and it urgently requested advice on "a line of action best calcu-

---

[19] *Engineering and Mining Journal* 69 (1900), 417, 702; 71 (1901), 491; 72 (1901), 36; *Pacific Coast Miner* 8 (1903), 393–94.

lated to bring about a reduction of this smoke." There is no record of any response by university officials.[20]

That July a frightening blaze roared through the smoke-dried brush and slash around the town of Shasta. There was another big brush fire the following September, in the horticultural district called Happy Valley, centered on the town of Olinda. In both instances a wholesale destruction of property was averted only by extensive backfiring and a big turnout of hands. Forbearance was coming harder all the time to men who saw their lands and crops in daily peril. "Like a cloud upon his title the farmer must wait until the dread area of affection reaches him," commented one rancher. "In the meantime the value of his property is going, gone." The farms and ranches of Shasta County represented an investment of more than $3 million by this time, the best of which was concentrated precisely in the zone most affected by Keswick smoke. Orchards and other improvements were largely the work of the present generation and were just getting to be on a paying basis. Impatient with the slow progress of the government's suit, farmers contemplated bringing actions of their own against the Mountain Copper Company.[21]

English and American case law had always recognized that covering a neighbor's land with noxious smoke and vapors was an invasion akin to trespass, subject to injunction at the suit of the injured party. "Indeed," a contemporary treatise declared, "it may be said that no one has a right to interfere with the supply of pure air that flows over another's land any more than he has to interfere with that neighbor's soil." And, according to the hornbooks, neither the general importance of the offending business, nor the amount of capital invested

---

[20] *Redding Free Press*, March 15, November 13, 1901; June 9, 1902.

[21] Ibid., August 2, 1901, September 11, 1902. See also Lapham and Holmes, *Soil Survey of the Redding Area, California.*

in it, nor the number of people benefited by it, would constitute a valid defense to such a complaint. The rights of
habitation—so ran the law's ancient principle—were always
superior to any rights of commerce. "Where justice is properly administered," the Supreme Court of Pennsylvania intoned in an 1880 smoke case, "rights are never measured by
their mere money value, neither are wrongs tolerated because
it may be to the advantage of the powerful to impose upon
the weak."[22]

In actual practice, however, these controversies were sel-
dom so clear-cut. Lack of firm scientific knowledge about the
pathological effects of sulfur dioxide and other fumes and
gases made the problem of proof extremely tricky and gave
defendants many opportunities for obfuscation and denial.
What was more, local judges and juries were extremely reluctant to decide against an industry that was a fountain of
employment, revenue, and commercial opportunity. Stephen
Lavender relates the story of an important smoke trial decided at the Carmarthen Assizes in 1833, when the country
landowners of Llansamlet Parish, Wales, sought an injunction against the big Haford Copper Works at Swansea. The
farmers complained that the clouds of "copper smoke"
thrown off by the Haford smelter made them, their families,
and their livestock seriously sick; that the sturdy groves of
oak, ash, and sycamore that once graced the neighborhood
were all dead and gone; that once-excellent corn, hay, and
pasture land was forced to lie untenanted and barren. The
company's high-priced barrister argued that "such effects
were as likely to have followed from bad land and worse culture," that the failure of crops was due to common blight,
"which, like the copper-smoke, affects the blossom," and that
cattle in places far removed from any smelter "became some-

---

[22] Wood, *A Practical Treatise on the Law of Nuisances*, vol. 1, 677; "Appeal of the Pennsylvania Lead Company," 127.

times the subject of diseases not unlike those said to be caused by the copper-smoke." And he eloquently drove home the importance of smelting to the growth and prosperity of Swansea and its suburbs. A verdict immediately was returned in favor of the smelter. "The news has diffused the greatest of joy throughout this neighbourhood," the local newspaper exulted. Practically the same obstacles faced by the Welsh farmers in 1833 confronted their counterparts in California sixty-eight years later.[23]

In October 1901, the proprietors of a fifty-acre orchard in the hills just three miles from Keswick brought suit in Shasta County's superior court, asking damages of $15,000 and, what was bolder, an injunction that would stop the company from smelting unless it could contain the noxious elements of its smoke. Peter Stolberg and his partner complained that smelter smoke had withered twenty-five hundred young almond trees and rendered their property unrentable and useless. Mountain Copper paraded a dozen witnesses averring that the partners' trees had been scotched by frost, not fumes, and that almonds could never succeed on their land anyway. The complainants maintained that there was no excuse for letting the damage go on, because the sulfurous gases could be captured and condensed by the company and profitably utilized in the manufacture of sulfuric acid and artificial gypsum, products that could be absorbed in limitless quantities by the alkali and adobe lands of the state. Blackboard demonstrations by the company's fast-talking experts persuaded the court of the technical and commercial impracticability of that idea. The company's attorneys, led by the president of the San Francisco Bar Association, briskly dissected the inconsistencies in the farmers' contentions and repeatedly stressed the magnitude of the interest at risk, a

---

[23] Lavender, *New Land for Old*, 43–49. See also Rees, *King Copper*, 76–89.

great enterprise distributing over a million dollars a year in the region, whose closure would be disastrous to the whole county and indeed the whole state. An emotional wind-up by the farmers' attorney, with histrionic references to British imperialism and the valiant struggle of the Boers, availed little. A compromise verdict ended up giving the partners $645 for their losses—all of which and then some was promptly attached by their lawyers, stenographers, and expert witnesses. Their request for an injunction was refused. The outcome of California's first smoke trial was a telling preview of future contests.[24]

Frustrated ranchers wrote to officials in charge of the federal government's injunction suit, asking about the status of that case and protesting the slow progress of litigation. They were advised that an offer of compromise had been made by the company, and until it was either accepted or rejected, instructions were not to press the case in court. "You have my sympathy in the matter," the U.S. attorney replied from his San Francisco office. "Of course, you will understand that representations are made by the Company that the mineral exploitations and developments now going on afford employment to thousands of men, and are of much more financial benefit to the country at large than the damage done to the residents, fruit-growers, and farmers in the immediate vicinity." And he followed with a remark that must have seemed damnably obtuse to farmers in the wake of the recent smoke trial in local court: "Furthermore, the Company, as I understand it, professes to be willing to remunerate those who have been damaged."[25]

A committee of fruit-growers decided to try a direct appeal to the highest law officer in the land. "The Interior Department," they informed President Theodore Roosevelt in

---

[24] *Redding Searchlight*, November 12–16, 20–23, 1901; February 8, March 23, 29, 1902.

[25] Marshall B. Woodworth to George A. Lamiman, April 29, 1902, in DOI 5451-1897.

a homespun manifesto, "is laboring under a misrepresentation in regard to the amount of Government land affected and the serious injury that is being done to homes that represent years of toil and sacrifice." They told of a hundred homesteads "destroyed by a foreign corporation that boasts of a net profit of over three millions. All of which would be available and if necessary used against our Government while the victims of their greed would be expected and in all probility would rush to their country's support." After explaining the situation they were up against they entered their "most solemn protest against any compromise," and went on to suggest a strategic partnership:

> We can furnish all the evidence you may desire to show that the timber on Government land is being destroyed for twenty miles from the smelter, by reason of which, several have abandoned their homesteads and other good property is unclaimed, while some who have developed their homesteads refuse or hesitate to apply for a patent. Also, that by reason of the destruction of the timber on mineral land, the poor man is unable to develope a mine and it works a monopoly for the foreign company. A principle which is surely inimical to republican institutions. [26]

"By taking care of the Government's property, you will save a worthy and patriotic people," they reminded Roosevelt. The investment community watched this rise of farmer activism and voiced its irritation in pretty coarse terms. New York's *Engineering and Mining Journal* dismissed the agrarians as nothing more than avaricious pikers, "people with little $500 orchards," anxious to get in a champertous whack at a large and prosperous corporation. "Disgruntled mossbacks and thrifty blackmailers," a San Francisco mining weekly called them. The county, it remarked, would do well to condemn the holdings of the mal-

---

[26] Z. T. Stroup and S. W. Landon to Theodore Roosevelt, July 26, 1902, in DOI 5451-1897.

content settlers and move them out. The *Los Angeles Mining Review* denounced the yokels' "nasty antagonistic demeanor" and thought it "incomprehensible" that the progressive and enterprising majority in Shasta County would encourage by its silence, "or permit at all," any attempt to impose a "great hardship and unnecessary expense" on the region's leading industry. "We do not drive away business enterprise from the Southland; we encourage them to come and make it pleasant for them to stay."[27]

Meanwhile, the U.S. General Land Office had finally reached a conclusion on the copper company's offer to exchange its forest land holdings in Kern County for title to the smoke-damaged public lands around Keswick. The office's investigation showed that the lands the company sought to acquire were neither nonmineral nor vacant as the law required, being strewn with numerous unpatented lode and placer claims. It also was determined that the company's application had failed with regard to various technicalities of filing and public notice. The application accordingly was rejected, and the commissioner of the General Land Office duly reported that there was nothing more to prevent vigorous and decisive action on the long-pending suit. The secretary of the interior immediately requested the Justice Department to "prosecute this important case to a conclusion."[28]

Both departments complained of being short-handed and short of funds, however, delaying action on the suit for most of a year. The preparation of the case also seems to have been hampered by a certain ambivalence or half-heartedness on the part of those in charge. The commissioner of the General

---

[27] *Engineering and Mining Journal* 75 (1903), 234; *Redding Free Press*, July 18, August 1, 1904; *Mining and Scientific Press* 88 (1904), 358.

[28] Commissioner of General Land Office to register and receiver of Redding Land Office, April 8, 1902, in GLO 30; acting commissioner of General Land Office to secretary of interior, August 9, 1902, and acting secretary of interior to attorney general, August 11, 1902, in DOI 5451-1897.

Land Office wondered whether the values at stake in the suit were really enough to justify the expenditures that would be involved in prosecuting it. Solicited for a report and opinion, Director Charles Walcott of the U.S. Geological Survey replied, "It does not appear to me that the damage to vegetation produced by the sulphur fumes can be a serious matter, certainly not at all compared to the destruction of this industry." A special agent sent out to collect evidence also betrayed a shielding attitude toward the smelter: "Since my arrival here I have fully satisfied myself that an action for an injunction should never have been brought and that much time and unnecessary expense has been wasted. . . . The lands of the Government are mountainous lands and the injury consists in the destroyal of the scrubby scattering and almost valueless growth of trees on same by the fumes." An injunction against the company would force enormous hardship on "the nearly thousand employees and their families who are connected with their works and would inflict much injury upon the business and inhabitants of the surrounding towns." Most of the serious damage was being sustained by local farmers, Special Agent Parke concluded, and they could pursue their own remedy in local court if need be. Its manager had assured him that the company "amicably settled" all "reasonable" complaints brought against it.[29]

The price of copper tumbled in 1902, and the Mountain Copper Company sharply cut back its operation in response. That fall a major strike erupted which kept the mine and smelter idle all winter. The company brought up strikebreakers in February 1903 and got two of its blast furnaces going, but the sheriff's men were not withdrawn from Keswick until May, and aftereffects of the disturbance ham-

---

[29] Commissioner of General Land Office to secretary of interior, May 4, 1903, and director of Geological Survey to secretary of Interior, October 17, 1903, in DOI 5154-1897; F. J. Parke to commissioner of General Land Office, March 21, 1904, in GLO 30.

pered operations all summer. Production and profits in 1903 were only half what they had been in 1901. The copper business had recovered its stride by the spring of 1904, however, and the Keswick plant was again running full-handed, treating twenty-six thousand tons of ore a month. The revival of smelting coincided with a disastrous year for fruit. Statewide the 1904 prune crop made a high average, but Shasta County's was almost a complete failure. The market also was in a state of confusion set off by the recent bankruptcy of a large marketing association, and county growers found themselves getting little more than a penny a pound for their staple. The return from the peach crop was almost as dismal.[30]

Many farmers were driven to the conclusion that they could not afford to let uncompensated injuries accumulate while they patiently waited for the federal government's injunction suit to resolve itself. Some of them decided to try their luck in county court one more time. Eight small orchardists banded together in October 1904 and sued the smelter for $34,500 covering damages incurred since 1902, all the statute of limitations would allow. The plaintiffs occupied good bottom lands along the Sacramento River just above Redding, hardly five miles from the smelter. They said the heavy smoke from Keswick shrouded their properties like fog many days, trapped by the high bluffs that flank the river in this section. Peach and plum blossoms shriveled; alfalfa, oats, and garden vegetables blanched and drooped over. The company completely rejected the farmers' claims, saying their losses were due to frost injury and other natural causes, aggravated by "improper care." The trial was opened by Judge Charles Head in January 1905 and lasted ten days.

[30] *Redding Free Press*, November 20, 1902; February 6, 16, May 3, 1903; August 19, 1904; *Engineering and Mining Journal* 74 (1902), 761, 826; 75 (1903), 494, 534, 942; 77 (1904), 135, 659.

The farmers came to court armed with weather and crop records, sprigs of injured vegetation, and years of close personal observation of Keswick smoke and its effects. Their testimony showed that they were only too familiar with the peculiar bleaching and burning produced by sulfur dioxide, and they had no trouble detailing the ways it differed from frostbite. The lead plaintiff, Perry Mark, had lost almost his whole orchard to smelter fumes, a planting that originally numbered twenty-five hundred trees. He had been on his place for twenty-five years. He told how blue-ribbon fruit crops, consistently full in the old days, had dwindled to almost nothing after 1898; how new growth wilted and blossoms refused to set; how once-robust trees lost vigor and became sunburned as they fell victim to repeated defoliations during the growing season. "I cultivated and pruned my orchard in the best manner that I knew how," he said ruefully. "I did the very best work that I could." The gray pines on his property also were dying off, and even the tough manzanita bushes were showing the ill effects of smelter smoke. "They are the natural growth of the country," he pointed out. The native oak trees were bearing scarcely any acorns, and the heavy crops of mast he once relied on for feeding his hogs had practically ceased: "I do not believe you could pick up a full sack of acorns on any fifty acres there." Mark had plenty of local witnesses to back up his statements.[31]

On the sixth day of the trial the county sheriff seated judge and jury in a four-horse hotel bus for a field trip to the plaintiffs' farms. The *Searchlight* could not help but smirk at the proceedings. "The attorneys for the Mountain Copper Company were good providers," furnishing jurors and court offi-

---

[31] "Statement on Appeal," January 31, 1906, in Civil Case File 3120, Shasta County Superior Court, Shasta County Clerk's Office, Redding, Calif.

cers with box lunches and a casket of fine cigars. Beer and wine also had been ordered, but Judge Head drew the line and that particular facet of corporate hospitality was re-strained. The juridical picnic party spent all morning and part of the afternoon viewing the properties at issue. When they got back to the courthouse they listened to the conclu-sions of the smelter's star witness, Edward J. Wickson, in-coming dean of agriculture at the University of California, who spent the rest of the day enlightening them on every reason besides smelter smoke for the impoverishment of the orchards—gravelly soil, an unfavorable climate, backward farming practices. Cross examination brought out the fact that Professor Wickson had been in the neighborhood at least three times before as a guest of the Mountain Copper Company. When he came to testify against the farmers in the Stolberg case in 1901 he had been paid $240 plus ex-penses. For making two tours of inspection the previous fall, after the filing of this suit, he had gotten $125 per trip, each made in a single day. A little further questioning revealed that his professor's salary at Berkeley was $250 a month. "But I don't sell all my time to the State," Wickson added, antic-ipating the next question.[32]

Testimony on the smelter's behalf occupied several more days and probably was quite superfluous, for when the time came the jury took just five minutes to bring in a verdict against the farmers. Judge Head stuck the astonished plain-tiffs for the company's itemized costs besides—over four hun-dred dollars, not including Professor Wickson's gratuity. Agriculturists all over the county had hoped this smoke trial would finally bring the smelter to account, and their dudgeon over the outcome was rather intense. A frustrated crowd in Happy Valley held a protest meeting on the main street of

---

[32] *Redding Searchlight*, January 11, 1905.

Olinda the following Saturday. They strung up and burned an effigy of a county horticultural commissioner who had taken the stand for the company, denounced him as a traitor and a grafter, and started a petition drive to abolish his office as a waste of public money. Also a movement was set afoot to unseat Judge Head, with open charges that he was "subject to improper influences."[33]

A measure of consolation came to the sulking farmers in March 1905, when federal judge William Morrow unexpectedly granted the U.S. government's request for an injunction against Mountain Copper. The company immediately posted bond and notified the court of its intention to appeal the decision, and Judge Morrow granted an indefinite stay of proceedings. Caught by surprise and thoroughly shaken, Redding people were sure the federal government would have been willing to relent and peaceably compromise its suit had the controversy not been fanned by "the outcry from irresponsible parties"—clearly meaning the unrelenting stream of complaints and petitions from local farmers. "The company has been sued and harassed by many individuals and combinations in Shasta County and from the time of its inception has been made the target of abuse by persons who come properly under the head of knockers," scolded the *Free Press*. A subscriber's letter expressed a more sensitive and compromising view of the situation. "We do not believe that millions of capital should be laid up inactive and rendered unproductive simply because a few hundred or a few thousand fruit trees and a township of scrub timber have been killed," wrote Lincoln Braden, a well-known local Socialist. "Believing this, we yet contend that the Mountain Copper Company, like any other company or individual, should pay the full

[33] Ibid., January 13, 15, 19, 27, May 12, 1905.

amount of damage it has inflicted upon adjacent property; and no plea of benefit to the community at large, and no threat of removal, should blind the eyes of this community to the fact that many homes have been ruined by the Keswick smelter fumes, while few have been paid for."[34]

Friends of the smelter received another jolt soon after, when news came that an aggressive district attorney two hundred miles south in Solano County had filed a lawsuit in the name of the People of the State of California, seeking a permanent injunction against an important lead smelter and precious-metals refinery operated by the Guggenheim syndicate on Carquinez Strait, at the northeast corner of San Francisco Bay right across from the Solano County town of Benicia. "It is a case of Selfishness vs. State Prosperity," wailed the *Redding Free Press*. "A feeble cry from a narrow-minded community to kill the goose that lays the golden eggs—to destroy the smelting industry in California—to drive invested capital from the State." Such black hand, knife-to-rib tactics should be discountenanced by "every public-spirited citizen," the paper warned, under the caption "Also Applies to Shasta." In another column, an article obtained on exchange gave a glimpse of what it was the "knockers" of Solano County were protesting. Within a radius of fifteen miles around the works of the Selby Smelting and Lead Company, this item explained, "the pasture lands have become arid and unproductive, while cattle turned out to graze on them die within six weeks. Horses seem to be the most easily affected; they at once commence to roar and suffocate. Their limbs lose all strength and after the first week or so it is impossible for them to travel fifty yards without falling." One prominent Benicia farmer had lost thirteen good workhorses this way.

---

[34] *Redding Free Press*, March 14, 22, 1905.

He had just one colt surviving, and it too was beginning to show symptoms.[35]

The Selby smoke trial got under way the following summer. Assayers for Solano County presented indisputable evidence of widespread contamination by lead and sulfur fumes. Selby's head metallurgist was interrogated about stack losses and admitted that the smelter's furnaces had been throwing off more than a ton of lead fumes every day, while hundreds of gallons of highly corrosive sulfuric acid mist escaped from the giant parting pots where crude bullion was boiled. A long line-up of Benicia people testified about the frequency and character of smoke visitations. They told how almost everyone was bothered with smarting eyes and sore throats when the Selby smelter fumes rolled in, how some suffered graver symptoms including headache, nausea, and a sense of suffocation. Most alarming was the smoke's baneful effect on horses in and around the town. Horses in good, slick condition when brought into the Benicia atmosphere would rapidly lose strength, grow short of wind, and develop various twitchy afflictions. After moderate exercise a "smeltered" horse would fall down and throw itself for breath, foaming and bleeding at its nostrils. More than one citizen had witnessed animals in such condition drop and expire right in the street. The smelter people suggested it was anthrax or some other infectious disease. The state veterinarian, Dr. Charles Keene, appeared for the county and confirmed that the unusual trouble was caused by the combined effects of lead, arsenic, and sulfur fumes.[36]

---

[35] Ibid., March 15, 18, 1905. See also, for example, Civil Case Files 3017, 3074, and 3090, Solano County Superior Court, Solano County Archives, Fairfield, Calif. Seeking cheaper land and deeper water, the Selby concern only recently had expanded its operations at the Carquinez site. For more than thirty years it had been the city of San Francisco's leading industrial interest, parrying smoke complaints from year to year with, among other things, the defense that it was after all operating in North Beach, an "uncivilized" (i.e., immigrant and proletarian) part of the city. See, for example, San Francisco Call, August 8, 22, 1876.

[36] "Transcript on Appeal," February 13, 1910, 79–249, 514–17, in CSC 1847.

The farmers of Benicia Township were especially bitter about their loss of livestock, the repeated spoiling and contamination of their hay crops, and the long-term poisoning and deterioration of their lands. Some gave significant testimony in this trial; many had damage suits of their own pending. They and the rest of "The People" were rudely surprised when some well-known faculty members from the state university took the stand on the smelter's behalf. It was not forgotten that Solano County had applied to numerous University of California professors for help and advice in preparing its case, but its requests either went unanswered or brought the reply that employees of a state establishment had to stick to a "strictly neutral position." President Benjamin Ide Wheeler of the university squirmed when he was later confronted about this, offered some sententious remarks about his institution's "judicial attitude," and conveyed assurances that the "whole attitude" of the professors "was and is one of non-partisanship" and that their testimony would have been "equally at the disposal" of either side. "Simply rot," cried one farmer, who plainly knew nothing of academic couth even if he had gained an inkling of academic corruption. "Is it not a case of being 'judicial' for the smelter alone? Or does the smelter's money cut any figure?" One of the smelter-suborned savants, Winthrop J. V. Osterhout of the university's botany department, had told the court that all farmers in the Benicia smoke zone had to do was learn to perform their work "more intelligently."[37]

Rendering his opinion in October 1906, Judge L. V. Harrier of the Solano County Superior Court decided that evidence of a serious state of nuisance was clear and convincing, forming indeed "a wall of direct testimony which could not be directly attacked." Concerning the pile of ex-

[37] *San Francisco Chronicle*, September 15, 1906; *Benicia Herald*, October 12, 19, 1906.

pert countertestimony presented by the smelter he said: "All they could prove was that the witnesses for the plaintiff were wrong in accepting the evidence of their senses, that they were not affected as they thought they were, for there was nothing in the air to affect them. I would have to say that the banker, the farmer, the tanner, the blacksmith, the fisherman, the editor, the housewife, and the forty others who testified as to their personal experience and their observations were all dishonest or laboring under one grand universal hallucination." Judge Harrier granted an injunction but qualified it by insisting that the "great enterprise" be treated with the "greatest patience," and he advised "great liberality" in insisting upon the execution of the injunction. Patience and liberality were terms that would acquire a notable irony as time dragged on.[38]

The Selby company promptly settled the twenty-five damage suits pending against it, but the question of Solano County's injunction was doomed to travel in circles for many years. The smelter proceeded to install various appliances for controlling its smoke, but success was only partial and serious complaints continued. Time and again Benicia citizens badgered their county officials for a final resolution of the problem, but the Guggenheims' seasoned legal staff proved to be exceedingly deft at raising quibbles and discovering loopholes. Meanwhile the smelter management had set detectives and technical experts to work assembling a platter of "newly discovered evidence," in an effort to force a new trial. Essentially, this was nothing but an elaborate attempt to pin blame for the noxious fumes on various oil refineries and chemical plants situated farther upwind. The company's lawyers also tried a curious appeal to higher principles: "As civilization advances, the rights of individuals are in a measure sacrificed to the com-

---

[38] *Benicia Herald*, November 2, 1906.

forts and conveniences of the many. . . . We are convinced
that the public interests represented by the appellant in this
action are far greater than the public interests represented by
the people of Benicia and its contiguous vicinity." The California Supreme Court ultimately denied this motion, but the
blessings of the injunction somehow continued to elude Benicia and its smeltered inhabitants.[39]

In Shasta County, editors regularly preached on the vital
need to save the region's paramount industry from "legal cru-
cifixion," and compliant officials did their level best to stamp
out what was seen as a rising epidemic of "anti-smelterism."
In October 1905, Judge Head quashed a motion for a new
trial by Perry Mark and his neighbors. "In Shasta County it
has been continuous loss for the contingent-fee lawyer, and
the 'hold-up' industry is as dead as a mackerel," whooped a
Redding mining sheet. "We must not hamper great capital-
istic enterprises in their efforts to develop our magnificent
mineral resources," another paper moralized. Meanwhile,
local interests were keeping a worried eye on the status of
the U.S. government's injunction against the copper company. The same day Judge Head dashed the farmers' last hope
in county court, Mountain Copper's attorney took a group
of Redding's most prominent businessmen in tow and
rounded up the county board of supervisors, bidding them
all to sign a memorial to the federal appeals court in San
Francisco, declaring that the future welfare and development
of Shasta County absolutely depended on copper smelting
and that a decision upholding the Morrow injunction would
cause enormous distress. The commercial interest represented by the farmers was of no account at all, one of the

[39] Ibid., July 5, 10–11, 25, 1907; July 10, August 7, 1908; October 29, 1909; November 8, 1912; Civil Case File 2980, Solano County Superior Court, Solano County
Archives, Fairfield, Calif.; "Appellant's Opening Brief," July 26, 1910, in CSC 1847. See
also "People of the State of California v. Selby Smelting and Lead Company," 84–95.

earnest merchants was supposed to have remarked. "It is the mines. The mines will make us all rich."[40]

With opinion at the county seat so thoroughly dominated by the smelter and those profiting by it, one disgusted farmer observed, it was no wonder that plaintiffs in smoke damage suits were doomed to lose their cases in local court. The Mountain Copper Company had "smoked us, laughed at us, and spit upon us," and now, faced with decisive action by a power it could not bully or defy, it scuttled around "running a big sympathy movement with the public." The company well knew that if it could secure the dissolution of the U.S. government's injunction it would be accountable to "no authority but its own pleasure" as to the quantity and quality of fumes it turned loose. Then it would have only local farmers to challenge it, who, suffering loss of crops and depreciation of property year after year, soon would be unable to undertake the expense of bringing new suits, "especially in view of the fact that they are sure to be turned down at home." But why should the smelter be placed above the obligations of common law and common responsibility, he asked. The agricultural community really was not hostile to mines or miners; it only asked for fair play and equity—"no smoke, or harmless smoke, or prompt payment of all damages caused by harmful smoke." And if a just settlement between the estranged interests could not be arranged by local government, the farmers' position on Uncle Sam's case could only be, "Let the injunction stand."[41]

---

[40] *Redding Searchlight*, October 19, 1905; *Redding Mineral Wealth*, February 15, 1906.
[41] *Redding Searchlight*, October 25, 1905.

CHAPTER TWO

"The right of the Government to equitable relief"

In the spring of 1903 the U. S. Department of Justice finally took steps to prosecute to a conclusion its long-pending suit against the Mountain Copper Company. It was prodded forward by the Department of the Interior, which had been urging decisive action on the case for a long time, as well as by continuing protests from Shasta County settlers. Special agents were put in the field to locate witnesses and collect affidavits. John Haywood of the U.S. Department of Agriculture's Bureau of Chemistry was assigned to report on the nature and extent of smelter-fumes injury around Keswick, while Thomas Price, a well-known chemical and metallurgical consultant from San Francisco, was engaged to study the Keswick smelter with reference to possible smoke-abatement measures. The government's evidence was ready by October 1903.[1]

Lewis T. Wright, the company's resident manager, personally wrote the secretary of the interior that month in an effort to set matters "in their true perspective" before the blade came down. His letter previewed virtually all the arguments the company would submit in court. He said his company very willingly would have taken steps to condense its smoke "but cannot do so economically." In any case, the

---

[1] Commissioner of General Land Office to secretary of interior, December 4, 1902, and Marshall B. Woodworth to attorney general, April 13, 1903, in DOI 5154-1897.

damage already was done, all to vegetation that "never had any value," and the government would gain nothing by an injunction at this point except break up an industry "which circulates in the area in question very large amounts of money." "The disproportion between the damage done by the sulphur fumes and that which would be done by closing California's largest mine is so enormous," he concluded, "that we believe we can ask you to waive that portion of the suit which prays for a restraining order and to allow the matter to be adjusted in amicable conference." The company previously had offered the government a 4,700-acre forest tract in Kern County by way of compensation, and Wright said it still was willing to deed over this land in settlement of the government's claim. This overture was turned down by the Interior Department and the company was duly informed that the case had been set for trial.[2]

"It is a fair and reasonable demand on the part of a sovereign," wrote Justice Oliver Wendell Holmes of the U.S. Supreme Court in 1907, "that the air over its territory should not be polluted on a great scale by sulphurous acid gas, that the forests on its mountains, be they better or worse, and whatever domestic destruction they have suffered, should not be further destroyed or threatened by the act of persons beyond its control, that the crops and orchards on its hills should not be endangered from the same source." In that case the state of Georgia obtained a federal injunction against the Tennessee Copper Company, whose smoke was drifting across the border from its smelter at Ducktown, Tennessee, and in the complainant's words "laying the territory of the State in waste more surely and completely than could be accomplished by any invading army bent upon its destruction." The U.S. government

    [2] Lewis T. Wright to secretary of interior, October 6, 1903, acting commissioner of General Land Office to secretary of interior, November 16, 1903, and secretary of interior to Lewis T. Wright, November 21, 1903, in DOI 5154-1897.

invoked the same principle before the International Joint
Commission twenty years later, when it took the field against
the giant Consolidated Mining and Smelting Company plant
at Trail, British Columbia, on behalf of the smoke-plagued citizens of Stevens County, Washington. "The sovereignty and
jurisdiction of a nation is exclusive over its own territory and
the air space over its territory," the State Department declared
in its brief. "The United States has no less a right to exclude
the injurious sulphur dioxide smelter fumes coming from the
Trail Smelter than it has to exclude undesirable aliens, dis-
eased livestock, and weeds."[3]

But rather paradoxically, the federal government was unable to assert the same high right in its case against the
Mountain Copper Company. "In considering this case,"
Judge Erskine Ross would say, "it is important to remember
that the question to be determined is one between the
United States and the defendant company only; the government suing, not in its sovereign capacity, but as a
landowner, to enjoin alleged injuries to its property. . . . It is
the well-established law that, when the Government comes
into court asserting a property right, it occupies the position
of any and every other suitor. Its rights are precisely the same;
no greater, no less." The government was confined to the ordinary right of an ordinary landowner to sue for the abatement of a nuisance, unfortified by any special power,
responsibility, or standing as guardian or conservator of the
commonweal. "If other owners of land have been so injured
by the same or similar acts of the defendant as to entitle them
to an injunction or to any other relief," said Ross, "it will be
time enough to consider their grievances when they shall
properly bring them before the court."[4]

---

[3] "Georgia v. Tennessee Copper Company," 233, 238; Metzger, *Trail Smelter Reference*, 98.

[4] "Mountain Copper Company, Limited, v. United States," 629.

The law of nuisance, as it concerned this case, boiled down to the ancient maxim, *Sic utere tuo ut alienum non laedas*—every person must so use his property and conduct his business as not to injure or interfere with that of his neighbor. Where an artificial obstruction or annoyance came in conflict with an established property right, the annoyance had to give way, no matter how much it cost its promoter. The common law of England always had been quite strict about this. Referring specifically to any owner of a "smelting house," Sir William Blackstone, the eminent eighteenth-century jurist, laid it down flatly: "It is cumbent upon him to find some other place to do the act where it will be less offensive."[5]

Horace Gay Wood, a leading nineteenth-century American authority on the law of nuisance, summed up the traditional attitude of the courts in these terms:

> The fact that the discomfort arising from the nuisance, or the actual tangible injury to property itself therefrom, is in no measure commensurate with the pecuniary loss to the owner of the works producing the injury by having his works declared a nuisance, is in no measure a defense or a circumstance to be considered by either the court or jury. If a party has seen fit to erect works in the vicinity of others which may injuriously affect the surrounding property by reason of its noxious character or results, the penalty of his temerity is to be visited upon him, however severe the loss, or however much less the damage may be to his neighbor than to himself. The innocent are not to suffer, either in their property or comfort, for the promotion of another's interest or profit.[6]

In other words, no defendant could claim to be injured by being prevented from doing to the hurt of his neighbor something he had no right to do, and it made no difference that the value and importance of the neighbor's property was small compared to his own. As recently as 1880 the Penn-

---

[5] Blackstone, *Commentaries on the Laws of England, Book the Third*, 217–18.
[6] Wood, *A Practical Treatise on the Law of Nuisances*, vol. 1, 706–707.

sylvania Supreme Court had not hesitated to confirm an injunction against a smelter whose smoke and fumes were destroying a forty-six-acre farm in its vicinity, even though that
smelter was the biggest enterprise in the city of Pittsburgh,
producing indeed one-fifth of the nation's refined lead. Justice Isaac Gordon wrote: "The rule *sic utere tuo ut alienum
non laedas* is a most valuable one, and must be maintained if
our civilization is to be cherished and preserved, and it is not
at all to the purpose to answer the charge of a violation of
this rule that the defendant's works have been erected at a
great outlay of capital; that they are important to the public
at large, and give employment to many men."[7]

But there was another doctrine in equity jurisprudence
that instructed judges to use the injunction in nuisance suits
very cautiously and sparingly, lest on relatively trivial
grounds an important enterprise be crippled or ruined and a
large amount of invested capital be idled or lost. In certain
cases, this doctrine taught, it was proper to deny the injunction and limit the complainant to his "legal remedy"; that is,
to a cash settlement for actual damages suffered. This was
the so-called balance-of-injury rule, which said that a court
should take into account the comparative hardship to the
respective parties of granting or refusing an injunction, as
well as its direct and indirect effect on the well-being of the
general public. In another section of his treatise Wood explained the loophole this way:

> The true intent of a court of equity being to do justice between
> parties, it will not issue a restraining order except where the rights
> of the parties demand it, and in determining this question all the
> circumstances of location, the effect of the act claimed to be a nui-
> sance, and the effect upon the defendant's business and interests
> will be considered; and, while the usefulness of the business or its
> importance, magnitude, or extent will not in all cases prevent in-

---

[7] "Appeal of the Pennsylvania Lead Company," 127.

terference, yet, if the injury on the one hand is small and fairly compensable in damages and the loss to the other party would be large and disastrous, an injunction will be refused and the party left to his legal remedy.[8]

This obviously exposed the *sic utere* rule to a good deal of judicial interpolation and modification, tempering and "balancing" the rights of disputants according to the perceived circumstances of a given case. We may think of it as an allowance for the exercise of common sense. But increasingly the sliding scale was given to favor heavy industry and big capital, and before long the "phlegmatically optimistic system of formal reasoning," as Joel Brenner calls it, was torn to tatters "under the persistent pressure of ad hoc utilitarian demands." By 1886, four of seven justices of the Pennsylvania Supreme Court had no doctrinal qualms about compelling a Lackawanna Valley farmer to accept a major coal company's fouling of the creek from which he got his drinking water. The court sent him home without an injunction and also refused him any settlement for damages, reasoning that an award of money to one complainant might bankrupt the company if all similarly aggrieved landowners in the area took advantage of the precedent. Justice Edward Paxson wrote for the majority: "The trifling inconveniences to particular persons must sometimes give way to the necessities of a great community. Especially is this true when the leading industrial interest of the State is involved, the prosperity of which affects every household in the Commonwealth."[9]

It was on those fluctuating and contradictory doctrines that the case of the United States against the Mountain Copper Company ultimately hinged. The battle finally was joined in November 1903, when the U.S. attorney submit-

[8] Wood, *A Practical Treatise on the Law of Nuisances*, vol. 2, 1182.
[9] Brenner, "Nuisance Law and the Industrial Revolution," 433; "The Pennsylvania Coal Company, versus Sanderson and Wife," 162. See also Freyfogle, *The Land We Share*, 66–77.

ted affidavits from more than seventy Shasta County citizens, who stated that the destructive effects of the smoke from Keswick were "continually and materially increasing," warning that if the smelter was not restrained it would "inflict great and irreparable injury upon the entire community, and will destroy all the private farms and orchards, as well as all the trees and vegetation growing upon the public lands of the United States." According to these statements, the circle of smoke damage now extended at least twelve miles west of the smelter and up to twenty miles south. The injuries of the past winter had been especially bad, they claimed. Most of these affidavits had been signed by farmers, whose fields and orchards had suffered sorely; some were turned in by woodcutters, owners of small mining claims, and others who had reason to deplore the deterioration of local timber supplies. The lines of personal interest were, as we already have seen, very sharply drawn in this struggle and were exploited thoroughly by the contestants.[10]

The company countered with over one hundred affidavits from merchants, contractors, hotel keepers, and other financially interested Redding people, and also from numerous small quartz mine operators in the area who prospered selling fluxing ore to the smelter. These inspired statements assured the court that gardens, shrubbery, and shade and fruit trees in the region were not detrimentally affected by smoke but flourishing; that sulfur fumes were hardly noticeable anymore and everything was looking "fresher and greener" ever since the company quit the practice of treating its ore in "stink piles," as they called the old open-air roast heaps. The smoke-affected area clearly seemed to be shrinking, in the opinion of these people, and beyond a radius of four miles or so from Keswick the poverty of vegetation should be blamed on the frequent brush fires, not smelter fumes.

---

[10] For example, George Baker affidavit, June 1, 1903, in NDC 12633.

Above all the company's supporters stressed that any damage to brush and to trees that were little better than brush was trifling compared to the smelter's great benefits to the county at large. The constable of Redding Township averred that the timber on the land in dispute "never did have any commercial value." An injunction, the president of the Bank of Shasta County predicted, "will cause a great decrease in the actual and assessed value of property in a very large portion of Shasta County" and consequently "inflict great and irreparable financial loss upon thousands of people residing in said county." There were some amusing variations on the standard message of these affidavits. One Quartz Hill miner claimed that sulfur and arsenic fumes actually benefited fruit orchards by killing off codling moths and other insect pests. "I wish we had more smelter smoke." A Buckeye storekeeper opined that by clearing the land of worthless brush the smoke was opening up more and better pasturage for the ranchers.[11]

In January 1904 the government filed as exhibits the two major reports it had commissioned the previous summer. John Haywood of the U.S. Bureau of Chemistry had gone over the country around Keswick and found that severe injury to all forms of vegetation extended over an ellipse of approximately ten-by-fifteen miles surrounding the smelter. He assayed pine needles and oak leaves gathered at different points around the fringe of the injured zone and found an abnormal sulfite residue which he supposed had derived from sulfur dioxide absorbed from the polluted atmosphere. Controlled fumigation experiments with potted trees in his laboratory seemed to confirm his supposition and settle the forensic question of what was responsible for the devastation. Haywood also presented evidence that contradicted the Mountain Copper Company's claim that its ore was entirely

---

[11] For example, M. F. Eldridge affidavit, December 12, 1903, and C. C. Bush affidavit, February 1, 1904, in NDC 12633.

free of arsenic. His analysis of surface soil samples at several points near the smelter showed the cumulative arsenic fallout reaching as high as seventy-five pounds an acre.

Haywood's assay of several samples of Keswick ore showed that it contained 42 percent sulfur on average. As a chemist he knew that two pounds of sulfur dioxide gas formed from every pound of sulfur that was burned. Assuming that virtually all the sulfur in the ore was incinerated in the roasters, blast furnaces, and converters, he calculated that for every ton of ore worked up at Keswick, 1,680 pounds of sulfur dioxide were given off into the atmosphere. On that basis of calculation, every 6.3 tons of Mountain Copper Company ore released enough sulfur dioxide to pollute one cubic mile of air to the degree of one part per million, a concentration plant pathologists knew could injure vegetation severely under the right conditions. If the Keswick plant was smelting one thousand tons of ore a day, then every twenty-four hours it theoretically imparted one part per million of sulfur dioxide to 160 cubic miles of the atmosphere—enough, potentially, to flood a four-by-forty-mile area of land with a layer of phytotoxic air one mile deep. "According to the direction of the wind, all of this sulphur dioxide would be sent in a particular direction so that we can easily see how the damage can be seen for miles away from the smelter." Haywood concluded that smelter-fumes injury around Keswick "will continue and even increase its limits unless the fumes are condensed."[12]

The report of Thomas Price, the San Francisco chemist, addressed the possibilities of "condensing" (that is, scrubbing and desulfurizing) the Keswick smelter gases before they were turned loose in the atmosphere. Price had inspected the plant and had watched huge volumes of smoke and fumes rolling away with no effort being made to capture the byproducts. He denounced this state of affairs as a great waste

---

[12] John K. Haywood report and affidavit, January 4, 1904, in NDC 12633.

as well as a great nuisance. "There can be no doubt but that the fumes from the furnaces at Keswick can be collected and successfully converted into merchantable articles." Price advocated the manufacture of sulfuric acid as the most promising solution. He said the technical feasibility of condensing highly noxious sulfur smoke into highly useful sulfuric acid was "a well-known industrial fact," and explained that both the time-tested lead chamber process and more novel catalytic methods were available to the company at reasonable outlay. The acid could be utilized widely in metallurgy, petroleum refining, and a great variety of other industrial processes. Every year the nation imported hundreds of thousands of tons of pyrites from abroad for sulfuric acid manufacture, he said. "Sulphuric acid may be said to be really the basis of modern chemical industry." It could be mixed with common salt to produce hydrochloric acid and Glauber's salt, two products that also had many applications in modern industry. The acid also could be mixed with phosphate rock to create a high-quality fertilizer, an article that was becoming increasingly valuable to California farmers and fruit growers. At the time, Price said, the state was importing all its superphosphate fertilizer from abroad.

Even if possibilities for commercial utilization of the smoke should be ignored, Price advised, there still were a number of other ways to suppress the nuisance, or at least to effect a "considerable amelioration" of existing conditions. He said the sulfur oxides could be neutralized and washed out of the raw smoke by passing it up through towers filled with crushed limestone down through which fresh water trickled. He pointed out that a large deposit of limestone suitable for this purpose was located just a few miles up the Sacramento canyon. Price also suggested the relatively simple expedient of conducting the smoke through long flues up to a high stack on one of the nearby ridge tops, where, discharged into higher and brisker air currents, it would be more rapidly diluted and diffused.[13]

A long affidavit by Lewis Wright attempted to answer Price's statements. The smoke from every ton of ore smelted at Keswick would yield approximately a ton of concentrated sulfuric acid, Wright figured. This meant the plant would be turning out as much as one thousand tons of acid every day. All the factories of San Francisco could not absorb more than one hundred tons a day. The developed industrial market for sulfuric acid was in the East, but it could not be delivered there from Keswick at any realistic cost. Acid was not a safe or convenient article to ship long distances: it required special railroad cars that would have to be returned empty, and freight charges would amount to about three times what the acid could be sold for at its destination. Price's suggestion that the company could start making fertilizer at Keswick also was infeasible, Wright insisted. The closest known phosphate beds were in Tennessee, and the commercial value of the rock simply would not bear the cost of such long transport under present market conditions.

The vast quantity of unmarketable acid that would be generated at Keswick could not be stored in ponds or poured out on the ground, for leaching and runoff would presently carry it into the Sacramento River, poisoning the water, killing fish, "and doing infinitely more damage than the fumes could possibly do." The idea of neutralizing the smoke by putting it through limestone towers was also shortsighted, according to Wright, for it would result in great volumes of water impregnated with sulfite of lime, which also would thoroughly poison the river. So, Wright concluded, while it was quite true that it was technically possible to desulfurize smelter smoke, the prac-

[13] Thomas Price report and deposition, January 4, 1904, in NDC 12633. See also Hart, "Problems in the Utilization of Smelter Fumes," 625–26; compare De Nevers, *Air Pollution Control Engineering*, 340–44.

tical realities of the business were such that "the necessary result of ordering the condensation of the fumes would be to
close down the smelter permanently and to destroy the business conducted there." He reviewed at length the many benefits the smelter conferred on the country, the millions of
dollars in wealth it generated and the thousands of people it
supported. The U.S. government's "discrimination" against
the beneficent enterprise in this suit was "unaccountable,"
Wright declared. "The same difficulties attend the manufacture of copper throughout the world and nowhere except in
very small quantities and in favorable localities have any of
Prof. Price's suggestions proved feasible."[14]

In a case that featured more than one queer twist, perhaps
the highest irony was that the Mountain Copper Company
was laying plans to embark on sulfuric acid production in a big
way even as its general manager stood before a federal court ar-
guing the sheer impracticability of such a project. In fact the
operation's management had been contemplating the latent
profits in the increasing sulfur fraction of its ores for some time.
Mountain Copper's corporate cousin, the Rio Tinto Company,
already was using thousands of tons of its Spanish pyrites to
make acid. Indeed one of the classic maxims of the industrial-
ist worldview—"The civilisation of a country may be estimated by the extent to which it uses sulphuric acid"—is
attributed to Hugh Matheson, one of the founding fathers of
Rio Tinto and of Mountain Copper as well. It happens that
large volumes of sulfuric acid are used in ridding crude oil of
water and other impurities. The opening of major petroleum
fields in the San Joaquin Valley and Standard Oil's completion in 1903 of a pipeline from those fields to its new refinery
at Richmond on the northeast shore of San Francisco Bay furnished an opportunity Mountain Copper was primed and

[14] Lewis T. Wright affidavit, February 1, 1904, in NDC 12633. See also "Smoke Problems of California," *Transactions of the Commonwealth Club of California* 8 (1913), 487–92.

ready to grasp. In July 1904 the company purchased fifty-five acres at Bull's Head Point not far from Richmond, and by year's end had the site ready for erection of a major new chemical plant. From this point on the Iron Mountain property was going to be exploited primarily as a sulfur mine. Among the company's interesting future sidelines would be agricultural sulfur and superphosphate fertilizer, distributed far and wide under its "Mococo" and "Inferno" trademarks.[15]

The taking of testimony in the case of the *United States vs. Mountain Copper* was done in the summer of 1904 by special examiners at Redding and San Francisco. A great many of the government's witnesses were small farmers from the district called Happy Valley, which really was not a valley but a rolling, wooded plateau lying west of the Sacramento River, ten to fifteen miles due south of Keswick. About twenty years earlier, settlers had begun taking up pieces of government land here, opening patches in the live oak, manzanita, and buckbrush to plant peaches, grapes, and olives. They had established a moderately prosperous community of seventy-odd families on the gravelly red soil, with about two thousand acres cleared and planted to fruit trees. They thought probably five or six times as much land could be improved were it not for the discouragement of "copper smoke." New plantings were quickly doomed by the fumes and established orchards were dying back rapidly. Iron pipe, steel tools, and household tinware swiftly corroded in the unnatural atmosphere, they said. Window screens did not last a year, and galvanized fence wire was eaten up after just a few seasons of exposure. Witnesses knew of several cases where recent homesteaders had abandoned their claims because of the situation. The present year was the worst ever in their experience. Smoke injury was now

---

[15] *San Francisco Chronicle*, June 18, July 13, December 23, 1904; *Engineering and Mining Journal* 77 (1904), 731; 79 (1905), 738; Avery, *Not on Queen Victoria's Birthday*, 181; White, *Formative Years in the Far West*, 239–43; Kett, "Fifty Years of Operation by the Mountain Copper Company, Ltd.," 127–31.

appearing in localities fully eighteen miles south of the smelter, in places that had seemed exempt just a couple of years before. The company management had put them off repeatedly with promises and excuses but so far had not come across with any compensation.

Happy Valley settlers told how the country was green and flourishing back in the days before the smelter, the oaks, pines, and manzanitas all strong and leafy. Now the native timber was dying off, the underbrush was dull-colored and sickly, and grass and herbage were scantier all the time. They said the gray pines had been first to show the effects, turning yellow at the top then drying up and dying. "The pine trees in the smoke have scarcely no needles on them at all—those that are alive." They said this timber was far from worthless—it made excellent fuel wood, it had been milled for fence posts and pickets in the past, and more than one settler had curbed his well with laggings made from gray pine, or had used it for floor joists. The farmers recognized the slow, cumulative effects of sulfur dioxide as well as the unmistakable acute injury that occurred when "a good dose" of smelter fumes drifted down during wet weather, leaving the country looking "as though a hot blast or something had passed through there." The past season had witnessed several such episodes. One severe fumigation in February had burned off that year's stand of grass, another in April had destroyed much of the peach crop. The farmers rebuffed insinuations by the company's attorney that rainy weather often carried freezing temperatures in its wake: too often they had seen the same results when there was no question of frost.[16]

A number of people from the Shasta and Whiskeytown neighborhoods, three to six miles west of the smelter, were interrogated. They described even sorrier conditions. Witnesses who had known the country for thirty years or more

---

[16] "Transcript of Record," June 5, 1905, 72–113, in CCA 1203.

had seen a once-dense forest of live oak and gray pine almost
completely killed off by the fumes from Keswick. "The timber is all dead, fallen down, nothing but very small, scrubby
brush at the present time." Now the injury was showing up
several miles beyond Whiskeytown, reaching some tracts of
unquestionably valuable ponderosa pine timber. Still these
witnesses could only testify to what they had observed on
their own properties or travelling along the county roads.
Their opinions, however well-founded, were not the opinions of "experts." They were not credentialed plant pathologists and could not positively rule out other causes of forest
injury and decline. They had not gone over the land as timber cruisers, running lines and counting the dead and living
trees from year to year. And while what they had to say certainly supported the government's contention that smoke injury was no better and in fact was getting worse, their
testimony did not relate directly to the specific tracts of public land described in the government's bill of complaint.
"There is not among them a surveyor . . . or any one who directly testifies concerning any of the Government land described in the bill, or concerning the extent of its injury by
defendant," the lawyers for the copper company would say
triumphantly. "The material issues of the case seem to have
been studiously ignored by the Government in its proofs,
while it has permitted everybody in Shasta County who had
a prior grudge against the Mountain Copper Company to de-
tail his personal grievances on the witness stand."[17]

For its part, the company engaged a licensed engineer to

---

[17] Ibid., 160–87, and "Brief for Appellant," October 10, 1905, 3–4, in CCA 1203. Gray
or "digger" pine (Pinus sabiniana), one of the signature trees of the chaparral-scrub woodland association of the California foothills, is widespread in this area at elevations up to
ca. one thousand feet. Ponderosa pine (Pinus ponderosa), the area's main commercial timber, becomes dominant at elevations above ca. one thousand feet. The "natural" boundary is often unclear: see Griffin and Critchfield, The Distribution of Forest Trees in California,
87, 89; Bloom and Bahre, "Historical Evidence for the Upslope Retreat of Ponderosa Pine
Forest in California's Gold Country," 46–59.

carry out an exact survey of the lands in dispute. He determined that only 4,178 acres remained in federal ownership in the two townships specifically named in the government's complaint. About a quarter of that, including everything in one of the townships, showed "no perceptible injury" in his judgment. On those tracts affected by smoke he found that nearly all the usable timber, everything over ten inches in diameter, already had been cut down and removed years before. Of the scrubby stuff that remained, about half was dead while half still had some life in it. He said none of the damaged land ever was classified as supporting valuable timber, according to field notes of the General Land Office surveys conducted twenty-five years earlier. Not much ponderosa pine or Douglas fir ever grew down at that elevation, he explained, while the soft and branchy gray pine never was regarded as commercial wood, even if settlers occasionally used it "under stress of circumstances." All the region's good timber was situated some miles to the north, beyond the reach of Keswick smoke. He testified that in his opinion the area of smoke injury was lessening rather than increasing, having found indications that a fresh crop of undergrowth was starting to spring up over much of what he called "the old killed zone." What he had seen, no doubt, were the last efforts of crown-sprouting chaparral species to regenerate themselves before they expired forever.[18]

Testimony taken at San Francisco mainly focused on the chances of harmlessly diffusing the smoke by means of an extra-high stack. Edward Vigeon, foreman of Amalgamated Copper's giant Washoe smelter at Anaconda, Montana, appeared for the government and explained the system recently installed there, which he believed had "absolutely remedied" the smoke evil. Harried by damage complaints and threats of litigation from surrounding ranchers, his company had

---

[18] "Transcript of Record," 410–34, in CCA 1203.

erected a three-hundred-foot smokestack atop a high hill behind its smelter. Crawling half a mile up the hill was a big
brick flue enclosing a series of capacious dust chambers sep-
arated by baffle walls. Vigeon explained how the arsenic and
other poisonous metallic particles in the smoke settled out in
the dust chambers while the high stack projected the sulfurous gases into higher air currents where they were completely diffused instead of descending to earth in concentrated
puffs as before. He said the arrangement had proved to be "a
gainer" to his company "in lots of ways": it had terminated
the trouble with the farmers, and it was recovering an abundance of rich material that formerly blew off as fine dust and
was lost. It had worked at Anaconda, and Vigeon saw no reason why it would not be an effective remedy for the state of
affairs at Keswick.[19]

William D. Harkins, chemistry professor at the University
of Montana, was called to testify for the Mountain Copper
Company. He emphasized that the vaunted stack at Anaconda was far less effective than claimed. Harkins explained
that a smokestack no matter how high would do nothing to
alter the essential character of sulfur dioxide: the gas in-
evitably would go out the stack in the same concentration it
went up, undiminished in volume. The diffusion of the gas in
the outside atmosphere was bound to be very slow owing to
differences in specific gravity. Sulfur dioxide was more than
twice as heavy as air and still would tend to settle out more
or less in blobs as it cooled, only pushed a little farther by
the wind as it fell from a higher point. Thus a taller stack
would only serve to broadcast the damage over a wider area.
This, said Harkins, was what was happening now at Anaconda, where smoke injury was showing up on farm and for-

---

[19] Ibid., 267–87. See also "The New Flue and Stack at Anaconda," *Engineering and
Mining Journal* 76 (1903), 962–65; compare, Harkins and Swain, "The Determination of
Arsenic and Other Solid Constituents of Smelter Smoke," 970–98.

est lands miles away from the smelter, where it never had appeared before. As a matter of fact the smoke and fumes problem at Anaconda was a long way from being settled. Harkins
and his mentor, Professor Robert Swain of Stanford, were
then engaged as key witnesses for the plaintiffs in a major
smoke suit against the Washoe smelter.[20]

Finally came Lewis Wright to sum up the Mountain Copper Company's position on the smokestack question. Dis-
charging the fumes at a new and higher point would be
"distinctly dangerous," he testified. As things stood, the
Keswick smoke snuggled down in the trough of Spring Creek
canyon where it was slowly taken up by the atmosphere and
gradually diffused. A tall stack perched atop one of the ridges
would only throw the smoke over a wider radius of country,
to attack more distant and probably more valuable lands.
Wright forecast that just as in the case of acid manufacture
the proposed remedy would prove to be "worse than the disease." And once again he took the opportunity to impress
the court with the economic importance of the smelter: how
it had created a prosperous community in a region that before was "devoid of life and industry"; how it had elevated
Shasta County from nominal to first-rate standing as a mineral district; how its closure would bring unemployment and
deprivation to literally thousands of people.[21]

But the discomfiture of thousands of workers and dependents apparently was shrugged off as a mere incidental of
sound business strategy when Mountain Copper shut down
its furnaces at Keswick the following spring and moved most
of the machinery two hundred miles south to Bull's Head
Point. In March 1905 thirty-five heavy freight teams long
engaged in supplying the smelter with quartz fluxing ore

    [20] "Transcript of Record," 331–73, in CCA 1203. See also MacMillan, *Smoke Wars*, 83–
99; Formad, "The Effect of Smelter Fumes upon the Live-stock Industry in the Northwest," 237–68.
    [21] "Transcript of Record," 401–408, in CCA 1203.

found their contracts abruptly canceled. By May the Keswick plant was "silent as the ruins of an ancient Palestine city." Redding papers assured their panting readers that copper smelting was not about to flee the area—only in the distempered imagination of "persons who have an anarchistic antipathy to capital as a rule." There were other big deposits of copper ore in the region and other big interests poised to exploit them. In September 1904 it had been confirmed that a strongly financed Boston group with rumored links to Standard Oil had purchased the Mammoth mine, a cluster of twelve claims not far from the defunct gold camp of Kennett, on the river ten miles above Keswick. By February 1905 a new spur track was laid at Kennett and preparations for a new smelter were visibly under way.[22]

Mountain Copper did not relax its formal stance at all. "We say that this attempt of the Government to throttle this great industry is wanton and senseless," the company declared in its opening brief to the federal district court in January 1905. The business was being conducted with all due care, and testimony showed that there was no other way to operate the smelter that would do any less damage to the surrounding country. Nor could the company have selected a place for its operations more waste or remote than Keswick, amid lands that had no natural value for agriculture and no market value at all. "The evident fact is that the Government lands described in the complaint are granite mountains thinly clothed with digger pines, scrub oaks, and manzanita brush. They are worthless desert; the despised residuum of the public lands. For fifty-five years the Government has offered them for sale to all comers at $1.25 an acre, or to give them away to anyone who would live on them, and has found no takers." The injury to the public domain, insignificant in any case, was readily compensated

---

[22] *Redding Free Press*, September 14, 1904; January 2, February 17, 1905; *Redding Searchlight*, March 15, May 14, 1905.

in money which the company readily offered to pay. It was, the company insisted, unreasonable and inequitable to confront a "great industry" with the threat of a court-ordered closure, merely that "the utterly worthless scrub trees and brushwood which once grew near the smelter might in the course of years return."[23]

"We contend," replied U.S. Attorney Charles Fickert, "that the defendant has no right to impose a perpetual servitude upon the land of the complainant or that of others similarly situated." The government had not only a reasonable and equitable right to protect valuable lands from injury and destruction, but a constitutional responsibility to defeat what amounted to "an unauthorized appropriation of public property for private uses." It could not accept a state of affairs that would restrict future disposal of its land, leaving it vacant or confining its use to what the defendant's smoke would allow. And the copper company could not be allowed the power to confiscate neighboring public land for a dumping ground, merely upon promising to pay some undetermined indemnity from time to time. The company's contention that the detriment suffered by the United States and by private landowners in the vicinity did not compare with the benefits the public derived from the smelter's operation should not, Fickert insisted, avail as a defense. He pointed to federal judge Lorenzo Sawyer's 1884 decision which rang down the curtain on unrestricted hydraulic mining on California's Yuba River. "We are simply to determine whether the complainant's rights have been infringed," Judge Sawyer had written, "and if so, afford him such relief as the law entitles him to receive, whatever the consequence or inconvenience to the wrongdoers or to the general public may be." The smoke generated by the Keswick smelter, just like the debris

---

[23] "Brief on Behalf of Respondent," January 7, 1905, in NDC 12633.

generated by hydraulic mining, amounted to an unlawful invasion and obstruction of complainant's property, Fickert maintained. The granting of an injunction was mandatory under the circumstances, and the court should not be deterred by any cost or difficulty its decision might impose on the defendant. And if the copper company could not or would not comply, "it should in that event be compelled to cease its operations."[24]

Judge William Morrow of the U.S. District Court in San Francisco found for the government, granting the injunction prayed for and awarding costs of court to the United States. His decree was issued on March 24, 1905, perpetually restraining the Mountain Copper Company from roasting or smelting ore at Keswick without condensing or otherwise removing the sulfur and arsenic fumes. Morrow declined to file an opinion, however, and he suspended enforcement of the injunction until the case could be reviewed and a mandate filed by the court of appeals. The company was directed to post a $15,000 bond to cover any interim operation. The company promptly filed an appeal, a move that was expected to insure its plant against interference for at least a year or two more. Downcast local interests took heart from the reflection that "there are many loopholes in the law and more than one way to avoid the consequences of an injunction, even when issued out of a United States court." The *Redding Searchlight* blithely pointed out that Standard Oil had managed to side-step similar federal court orders for years without having its profits reduced in the least.[25]

"This decision," worried the *Redding Free Press*, "together with the constant knocking of chronic soreheads, is bound to

---

[24] "Brief on Behalf of the United States," December 24, 1904, in NDC 12633; "Woodruff v. North Bloomfield Gravel Mining Co., and others," 806. See also Kelley, *Gold vs. Grain*, 229–42.

[25] "Final Decree," March 24, 1905, in NDC 12633; *Redding Searchlight*, March 25, 1905.

have a bad effect on the other companies investing money in the county." But the other copper companies that were getting active in Shasta County at this time really showed no hesitation at all about plunging ahead under the shadow of the Morrow injunction. All spring and summer the Mammoth company kept over two hundred construction workers "busy as ants in a pan of molasses" at the site of its new smelter at Kennett. By April 1905 the excavations were finished and foundations were being laid, and a two-and-a-half-mile aerial tram back to the company mine was in the process of being erected. By August the smelter buildings were up and the heavy machinery was being installed. Mammoth blew in its first blast furnace in October and a second one a few weeks later. Kennett had the look of a veritable boomtown. Copper topped sixteen cents that fall; the *Boston Commercial Bulletin* sighed that "it would be impossible to conceive of a more healthy and satisfactory market situation." Quickening market conditions prompted another eastern group to enter the field in November, purchasing the partially developed Balaklala mine for a reported $600,000 and issuing $1.5 million in bonds to finance yet another big smelter in the Sacramento canyon.[26]

The Mountain Copper Company's appeal was scheduled for argument before the Ninth U.S. Circuit Court of Appeals at the end of October 1905. Fretful about the consequences an adverse decision would have on the forward momentum of local commerce and property values, a group of Redding businessmen got up a so-styled board of trade to "respectfully protest against any action by the courts that will cripple our mining interests and deny us that prosperity and growth to which we feel we are entitled as a community." This committee and the copper company's attorney took their con-

[26] *Redding Free Press*, March 15, April 20, August 4, October 27, November 3, 14, 17, 1905.

Mammoth Copper's smelter at Kennett in perhaps its proudest hour, ca. 1907. Three of planned five furnaces in commission; baghouse not installed yet. Taken from an old postcard. Photographer unknown. Frame 33 (CD 83), Photograph Collection ["Snapshots in Time"], Shasta Historical Society, Redding, California.

cerns to the county board of supervisors, sitting at an "extraordinary session" one evening. The compliant supervisors passed a resolution on the spot, declaring that enforcement of Judge Morrow's arrant decree would "tremendously retard" Shasta County, paralyze its business, impair its taxpaying power, and deprive thousands of workingmen of a livelihood there, while on the other hand the vegetation destroyed by smelter smoke was "of very little importance from a financial standpoint." They delegated the county district attorney to carry the memorial to San Francisco and address the appellate court on the matter. Some citizens of contrary mind got wind of the action and forwarded a remonstrance to the federal court, pointing out that the supervisors' statement did not issue from a regularly called meeting but an after-hours gathering in the barroom of one of the local hotels. The circuit judges, as it ended up, brushed aside both the memorial and the remonstrance. Observers nevertheless thought they saw indications that "the sympathies of the court were against the Government's case."[27]

Both sides had good reason to be nervous going into the hearing. The government had the decree of the trial court and the weight of Anglo-American legal tradition in its favor, still it could not be any too sure of its ultimate footing. Courts everywhere were increasingly willing to tweak old principles to accommodate big business. Just a year before, the Tennessee Supreme Court had decided against the complainants in a controversy that presented similar facts and almost the same questions of law. The case originated in the Copper Basin of Polk County, Tennessee, the notorious Ducktown district where two smelters comparable in size and character to the Keswick plant were in the process of creating the nation's most infamous man-made desert.[28]

The "murder of a landscape," as Edwin Way Teale characterized environmental developments around Ducktown, also involved the economic murder of many small property interests in the neighborhood. A collection of local hill farmers prayed the Tennessee court for an injunction against the smelters, saying that half the timber on their land already was gone, that their crops repeatedly were destroyed and soon their places would not support their families, that their families were suffering in health and comfort as well. The defendant companies did not bother to refute those claims, instead

---

[27] Ibid., October 18–19, 30, 1905; *Redding Searchlight*, October 19, 1905.
[28] Teale, "The Murder of a Landscape," 352–56; Clay, "Copper Basin Cover-up," 49–55.

pressing the point that they were employing twenty-five hundred men in their works, distributing hundreds of thousands every year in wages and purchases of supplies, and paying half the property taxes of Polk County. The court weighed the fate of six hundred acres of "thin mountain lands of little agricultural value" against the consequences of shutting down the Ducktown smelters, whereby "a great and increasing industry in the State would be blotted out, and all of the valuable copper properties of the State become worthless." After disposing of several side issues, Justice M. M. Neil came down to "the principle which is of controlling interest":

> In order to protect by injunction several small tracts of land, aggregating in value less than $1,000, we are asked to destroy other property worth nearly $2,000,000, and wreck two great mining and manufacturing enterprises that are engaged in work of very great importance, not only to their owners, but to the State, and to the whole country as well, and to depopulate a large town, and to deprive thousands of working people of their homes and livelihood, and scatter them broadcast. The result would be practically a confiscation of the property of the defendants for the benefit of the complainants. . . . We see no escape from the conclusion in the present case that the injunction must be denied.[29]

The transcript of the trial of *United States v. Mountain Copper Company* was prepared during the summer of 1905, and the two sides submitted new briefs restating the arguments they had presented to the trial court. The company insisted that its smoke had, "except for occasional and accidental overflows," already accomplished all the damage it could possibly do in the Keswick region. An injunction, it told the appellate judges, was by definition a preventive remedy and could not be applied retroactively, to restrain a threat which no longer existed. And not only would the precedent set by the Morrow injunction nip in the bud all future prospects for copper mining

---

[29] "Madison et al. v. Ducktown Sulphur, Copper, and Iron Company, etc.," 664, 666–67.

in Shasta County: it threatened to strike down the smelting business throughout the nation. "Nowhere in America is any desert so complete as to be entirely without vegetation, and the poorer the land the more certain it is to be owned by the Government. . . . If then this injunction shall stand it will not merely annihilate the appellant's great investment and the flourishing community it supports with all its streams of commerce, but it will destroy all other hopes of copper production in this State, and, so far as it can be invoked, throughout the United States."

Such "tremendous consequences" demanded that the government's right to an injunction be "closely scrutinized and clearly established." Before stopping a useful and beneficial industry, the court must take care to exercise an "orderly and reasonable discretion"—it must "consider all the circumstances" and "seek a just proportion between the cause and the consequence." Before crushing a profitable business, the court must take into account the importance of the business, the capital invested in it, and its influence on the prosperity of the surrounding community. "The rule of comparative injury is and always must be a settled doctrine in the law of injunction." Before shutting down the Keswick smelter, the court was bound to inquire:

> Will its abatement result in trifling injury to the defendant, or will it amount to practical confiscation of all its property? Will its abatement be an insignificant matter to the public, or will the injunction paralyze the activities of a great population? Will the injury to the plaintiff be as great in withholding as to the defendant in granting it? Will plaintiff in fact be injured at all? Can plaintiff be made practically whole by an award of damages? If such an award would not be full compensation to a landowner, is it not a recognized principle of society and government that the good of the individual must give way to the good of the many?[30]

---

[30] "Brief for Appellant," October 10, 1905, in CCA 1203.

Mountain Copper's claim that "it can destroy the property of others because it cannot do its business without destroying the property of others" had no legal standing at all, U.S. Attorney Robert Devlin replied, and whatever benefits the general public happened to derive from the company's operation did not enhance the company's rights or palliate its wrongs. In every practical sense the copper company operated solely for its own profit, and in no sense could it cloak itself with the status of a public utility. If the timber and grass on surrounding public land could be devastated at the company's pleasure, it might as well be held that it could go on and seize the land itself. It would be a "dangerous innovation" indeed if the court legitimized such an invasion by refusing the injunction in this case, Devlin wrote. It would amount to nothing less than a forced sale, a confiscation of national property for private use, a condemnation of a section of the public domain for the convenience of the Mountain Copper Company. And a cash settlement of the sort the company wanted the government to accept would neither redress the wrong nor protect against its repetition. On the contrary, it would entail an endless series of costly and vexatious lawsuits, with no clear-cut or expedient way to establish the day-to-day damages. "To say therefore that the injured party must resort to an action for damages, and must bring successive suits as successive injurious acts occur, and may not obtain an injunction to preserve its property from injury, is to deny all relief whatsoever."[31]

"Isolated rhetorical expressions to the effect that any invasion of right, no matter how small, must be prevented by injunction without regard to consequences, cannot be taken literally," Mountain Copper argued in its final brief. "Such a

[31] "Brief for Appellee," October 23, 1905, and "Final Brief of Government," November 27, 1905, in CCA 1203.

doctrine could not be enforced in civilized society. If it were the law, then any girl in Redding who finds her pet geranium turning yellow would have the absolute right to shut down our works and throw half the county out of employment in order to prevent further damage to her flower." By its stubborn insistence on a narrow interpretation of its rights, the U.S. government threatened to overthrow a perfectly lawful and highly productive industry, cast thousands of its citizens out of work, and cut off a rich source of revenue to itself. "No reported case can be found where so unconscionable a demand for equitable interference was ever attempted. The utmost malice of private litigants has never gone so far in their efforts to injure enemies, as the United States of America has been successful in doing for the destruction of its citizens and friends."[32]

A two-to-one decision against the government was handed down by the Ninth U.S. Circuit Court of Appeals on February 21, 1906. The majority opinion was written by Erskine Ross of Los Angeles, a reliable friend of corporate interests. "It is quite true that it is a maxim of the law that every one must so use his property as not to interfere with that of another," Judge Ross announced. "But, where one cannot use his own property at all without indirectly injuriously affecting the property of another, then the sound discretion of the court of equity that is appealed to to abate the nuisance is invoked, and should be wisely exercised. Indeed," he continued, "that the comparative convenience or inconvenience to the parties from the granting or refusing of the injunction sought should be considered, and that none should be granted whenever it would operate oppressively or inequitably, or contrary to the real justice of the case, is the well-established doctrine, and we need hardly multiply authorities to that effect."

[32] "Appellant's Brief in Reply," November 9, 1905, in CCA 1203.

Ross was particularly impressed by the Tennessee Supreme Court's reasoning in the Ducktown case, and he quoted Justice Neil's opinion at length. He accepted the Mountain Copper Company's contention that copper production represented "one of the most useful and necessary of employments," that the smoke-affected lands had been "practically worthless" to begin with, and that the various methods suggested to abate the smoke were "wholly impracticable"—indeed much of Lewis Wright's deposition was reprinted verbatim in Ross' opinion. The testimony of the numerous farmers the government had enlisted to bolster its case he brushed aside as irrelevant, "except in so far as it goes to show that the acts complained of by the complainant affect those persons in a similar manner, and, indeed, in a much greater degree." Judge Ross concluded:

> We have, then, the ownership in the complainant of a little over 4,000 acres of land within the damaged zone, mountainous in character, with little or no soil, practically worthless for agriculture or horticulture, upon which most of such trees and undergrowth as existed had, prior to the commencement of this suit, been killed by the fumes generated by the appellant company (for which it is, of course, liable in damages for whatever they may have been worth), and upon which but little more vegetation of any kind remains, susceptible of destruction. In view of these facts, about which there can be no question upon the record, can it be doubted that the maximum injury that can result to the lands of the complainant embraced by the bill is but a mere trifle in comparison to the loss inflicted by the injunction in question upon the appellant company and those dependent upon and benefited by it? And, such being the case, would it be a wise exercise of the sound discretion we are called upon to exercise to sustain such injunction? We are of the opinion that it would not be.[33]

Judge Thomas Hawley of Nevada dissented sharply, however, saying the injunction decree of the lower court was

---

[33] "Mountain Copper Company, Limited, v. United States," 629–43.

"correct, and ought to be sustained." From the facts presented, Hawley concluded that if the copper company was allowed to continue operating under present conditions "the effect will be to absolutely destroy all the growing trees still alive on complainant's land, and render the same entirely without any value." He declared, "No principle of law is better settled in the jurisprudence of this country than that in all such cases the owner of the land is entitled to the writ of injunction." The company's claim that it could not condense or otherwise render innocuous its smoke at profit to itself was no defense, and its proposal that the government should sell or otherwise accept a "just compensation" for the devastated land was something a court had no authority to order. Nor was the company's invocation of the balance-of-injury rule an appropriate defense under the circumstances. The rights of individuals and corporations "are never to be measured by their mere money value," Hawley insisted:

> Courts have frequently and correctly held that an injunction ought not to issue where the damage is slight or trivial. In line with these decisions I fully agree. . . . But, with the exception of the Ducktown case in Tennessee, they do not hold that, where the nuisance is of such a character as to destroy the substance of the complainant's property, an injunction should not be granted. . . . The pith, point, and substance of this whole matter is that where the acts of a party, whether individuals or corporations, wealthy or poor, destroy the substance of a complainant's estate, whether it be of great or of but little value, an injunction should be issued.[34]

Reviewing the trial transcript, disgusted Department of Justice officials recognized that the government's showing was much weaker than it should have been. There were suggestions of serious negligence in the U. S. attorney's handling of the case. The fact that the area of injury had enlarged to affect public lands beyond those described in the

---

[34] Ibid., 643–50.

original complaint, and the fact that much of this land was of interest to homesteaders, adapted to fruit raising and other valuable uses, were considerations that had not been given proper emphasis. Other important evidence and testimony had not been presented, the absence of which from the record might well prove fatal to the chances of an appeal. Nevertheless an appeal seemed necessary, not only to keep the government in a better position if it came to negotiating a cash settlement, but also for the sake of retrieving "an important principle—the right of the Government to equitable relief in a case of this sort."[35]

Notwithstanding its doubts about the eventual outcome, the Department of Justice perfected an appeal in July 1906, and prepared to push the case to a final determination before the U.S. Supreme Court. At this juncture the Mountain Copper Company expressed its readiness to settle, offering a lump payment of $5,000 to cover all damages and costs to date. The government rejected that sum as completely insufficient. After the case was docketed with the Supreme Court the company raised its offer to $25,000, provided the government drop its appeal. Justice Department officials regarded this proposition more favorably, at the same time reminding themselves that any deal of the kind meant that an important principle would be sacrificed, an important point of equity surrendered, and Judge Ross's adverse decision would be left standing "as a precedent which might give us considerable trouble in the future."[36]

Redding newspapers frankly rejoiced that the Morrow injunction was dissolved and "a very great stumbling block in the way of progress and prosperity for the county in general

---

[35] DDC, "Memorandum relative to MCC Case," June 19, 1906, in DOJ 5706-1898.

[36] David D. Caldwell, "Memorandum for Mr. Hughes," August 23, 1906, in DOJ 5706-1898; acting attorney general to secretary of interior, October 18, 1906, commissioner of General Land Office to secretary of interior, November 9, 1906, and secretary of interior to attorney general, November 15, 1906, in DOI 5154-1897.

has happily been removed." "The commercial sky has been overcast with the clouds of impending disaster," the *Free Press* editorialized, "and now the sun has rifted the clouds and the bright rays of future prosperity and success are brightly shining on this community." The *Searchlight* hoped that "henceforth there shall be sufficient liberality and enlightenment among our people to enable us to adjust our industrial interests and differences so as to avoid another such experience." *Mineral Wealth* summed things up more bluntly: "While the local interests have been disposed of in the county court, the effort to hamper the industry through federal injunction has also failed. . . . In fact, Shasta County has settled down to a fixed policy of welcoming the capital needed to develop the vast copper resources within her borders, and no smelting district of the West will be so free from annoying suits."[37]

"We are very much pleased over the matter and I can assure you the people of Shasta County should rejoice," Lewis Wright told the local press. "It is an important matter, not only to us, but to the smelting industry generally, and the people interested in copper mining will certainly share our elation." The furnaces at Keswick had been cold for almost a year and prospects were dim for a real resumption of activity there, but the federal appellate court's dismissal of the Morrow injunction had cleared the legal horizon for other, even bigger operations up the canyon. The Mammoth company blew in its third blast furnace at Kennett a few days after the decision was handed down, and in June 1906 the management disclosed plans to install two more furnaces as soon as possible. Underground work at the mine had revealed a larger and better body of ore than anticipated, and the company was eagerly acquiring other promising proper-

[37] *Redding Free Press*, February 26, 1906; *Redding Searchlight*, February 27, 1906; *Redding Mineral Wealth*, March 1, 1906.

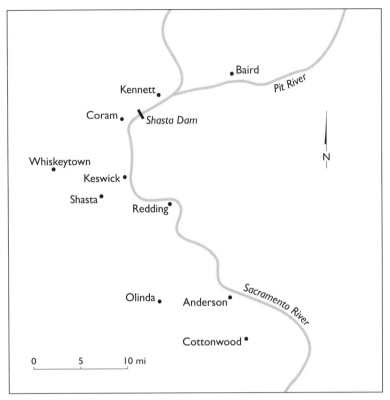

Map of the Shasta County, Califonia, "smoke belt." Scale 1:425,000.

ties in the neighborhood. Market conditions looked stronger than ever: copper crossed twenty cents that summer, national production was at an all-time high, and the *United States Investor* exclaimed, "The extent of the world's needs appears to be almost unlimited." The Balaklala company finalized plans for a big new smelter at a site three miles below Kennett, naming the place Coram after the Boston financier who had organized the company and still controlled the largest block of stock. Construction began in May 1906, and it was expected that the smelter would be in commission within a year. Fortified with a big infusion of Guggenheim capital, the company was pushing development work at its main mine as well as on nearby claims it had recently bonded.[38]

Interest in Shasta County orchard land also was picking up as fruit growers shipped a bumper crop at good prices, realizing over $400,000. The farmers' cheer was somewhat tempered by the prevalence of sunburn resulting from a mysterious, widespread defoliation that took place after an unseasonably cool, humid spell in July. On all species of orchard trees as well as the native oaks, healthy leaves suddenly had dried up and dropped off, "giving the face of nature a sort of midwinter appearance." It was an eerie portent of things to come. "Some of the calamity howlers have already rushed into notoriety and blamed Kennett smelter smoke for the premature falling of leaves," friends of the smelter were quick to say. But the smoke, "while we get a whiff of it occasionally," had nothing whatever to do with the freak phenomenon, they assured. The abnormal condition of the almond, peach, and prune trees was charged off to "red spider," that of the oaks was blamed on "hot weather coming so suddenly on the cold spell." Perhaps this was a satisfactory explanation to farmers who managed to have a good year regardless. The hated Keswick smelter no longer was puking its rank fumes, while the new Kennett plant was situated ten miles farther up the canyon—too distant, they fondly thought, to present much of a threat.[39]

Wall Street stumbled in the spring of 1907, and in the general strip-down that followed, the price of copper slid to thirteen cents, from its recent high of twenty-six cents. The fledgling Balaklala company was caught off balance finan-

---

[38] *Redding Courier-Free Press*, March 2, May 3, 14, July 6, 9, 26, August 17, 28, October 26, 1906; *Copper Handbook* 8 (1908), 349–51, 903–906. See also Martin, "The Mammoth Smelter at Kennett, California," *Mining Science*, pp. 205–206.

[39] *Redding Courier-Free Press*, July 23, August 22, October 26, 1906.

cially, had to lay off a large part of its mine force, and practically ceased work on its smelter for the better part of a year. Mammoth weathered the crisis better, kept its payroll intact, proceeded with the erection of a new 250-foot smokestack (double the height of the old one), and completed a four-mile railroad back to its mine, the ore-hauling capacity of the old aerial tram being inadequate to serve the planned enlargement of furnace capacity at the smelter. The plant's two additional blast furnaces were installed but their blowing-in was delayed pending an improvement in market conditions. Slack times in copper mining meant an extended respite from smelter fumes for county fruit growers, who brought in another banner prune crop in September and moved it at a record price. The prospects for local horticulture looked better than they had for a long time, and investors bought up an estimated $250,000 in developed and undeveloped orchard lands around Anderson that fall.[40]

The government's case against Mountain Copper still was not settled but it was getting closer. In negotiations that fall the company recast its offer to compromise in terms that seemed especially advantageous to the government. The company agreed to pay the United States $10,000 in cash and to convey title to the 4,750 acres still held in escrow in the Sierra Forest Reserve in Kern County. The land was to be taken at a nominal valuation of $15,000, but the government's attorneys were satisfied it was really worth at least $60,000. The Justice Department promptly approved the transaction and drew up articles of settlement, with no stipulations or restrictions at all on future smelting operations at Keswick. The department clearly was tired of the affair and did not care to introduce another source of complication or delay. The final agreement was executed on May 1, 1908, ten years and fifteen days after the government first

---

[40] Ibid., June 28, August 7, 14, October 14, December 5, 1907.

brought suit against the British corporation. The United
States accepted the cash and the Kern County land, and in
turn agreed that the 1905 Morrow injunction "shall not be
enforced" and "shall be held of no effect." It further acknowledged that the Keswick smelter fumes had "already accomplished all the damage they are likely to do," and
recognized that the Mountain Copper Company "may now
operate its Shasta County plant without further injury to the
timber."[41]

The Department of Justice was well aware that the
progress of this case was being followed closely by private
property owners near Keswick, who still hugged the delusion
that strong action by the federal government would rescue
them from a situation that looked more hopeless all the time.
Mountain Copper had overhauled two of its blast furnaces
and now was running one of them intermittently. As recently
as January 1908 a memorial from a group of Shasta farmers
had warned that the company was dragging out negotiations
only because "it is cheaper for the stockholders in London
to destroy the forests of the United States and the farms of
the American citizens than to condense the deadly fumes.
This corporation not only wants the earth but they also want
the air." They reminded the attorney general that their lands
too were being ruined and that they as individual citizens
were being pauperized, to a point where they had no money
left to pursue their own remedy in court. "Every one is entitled to the protection of the law in the use and enjoyment of
his property and if a foreign corporation is favored by special
privileges it will deprive us of our constitutional rights." "We
claim the same rights for our orchards as the London company claim for their mines," they sensibly argued. "The plant-

---

Charles T. Eells to Robert T. Devlin, November 11, 1907, WJH, "Memorandum in
Re United States v. MCC, Limited, No. 77, October Term, 1907," December 21, 1907, and
"Articles of Compromise and Settlement," May 1, 1908, in DOJ 5706-1898.

ing of our orchards not alone cost thousands of dollars, it also cost us hard labor to cultivate same and should we now leave it to the mercy of this wealthy corporation for destruction?"[42]

The Department of Justice kept quiet as long as it could about the accommodation it had reached with Mountain Copper, knowing very well that "many citizens will be undoubtedly displeased by this settlement." Yet the department unmistakably intended to distance itself from the farmers' plight. "The farmers," Attorney General Charles Bonaparte finally decided, "will have to seek their own relief in the state courts, should the operation of the smelter cause them additional injury." They accordingly were informed that the department had no authority to carry on proceedings for their protection and that it was wrapping up the case "as it deems proper for the protection of the interests of the United States, and without regard to interests not under its care."[43]

---

[42] *Redding Courier-Free Press*, March 27, 30, April 15, 1907; "The Committee" to attorney general, January 16, 1908, in DOJ 5706-1898.

[43] Attorney general to Peter Stolberg and F. C. Maurer, February 3, 1908, WJH, "Memorandum for the Solicitor General," September 12, 1908, and attorney general to R. T. Devlin, November 17, 1908, in DOJ 5706-1898.

The smelter at Kennett decomposing, 1935. Ruins of the plant's old baghouse extend up the hill behind rusting carcass of main facility, butchered for scrap eight years before. Photograph by D. M. Ilch. Image 306,227, Photographs and Research Data, Pacific Southwest Forest and Range Experiment Station, U.S. Forest Service, Federal Records Center, San Bruno, California.

CHAPTER THREE

"This part of California
is literally scorched"

The specter of a major business depression was haunting the nation in 1908, and Shasta County merchants and workingmen looked nervously to the local copper industry to shield and sustain them. In October the third anniversary of the Mammoth smelter was marked with speeches, ball games, and brass bands. The festive editorial in the *Courier-Free Press* could have been penned by George F. Babbitt himself. "Where," it demanded, "is the progressive citizen in the whole of Shasta County who would decry our magnificent mineral output? Where is the MAN who is a credit to his community who would say that Shasta County would be better without her great mineral reduction plants than with them?" The $40 million in copper produced in the ten years since a meddling government first brought suit against the old Keswick operation should, the paper crowed, be plenty to disabuse any "knocker" and prove the unequivocal blessing of outside capital coming in and "turning useless mountains into veritable mints and sections of industrial activity and progress."[1]

The new smelter at Coram blew in its first furnace a few days later, and the pillar of toxic smoke that could be seen all the way from Redding was hailed by the people there with

---

[1] *Redding Courier-Free Press*, October 17, 1908.

"great rejoicing," we are told. When it came to boosting, go-getting, and other cardinal civic virtues of the era, Redding's business leaders were assuredly second to none. With jealous pride they petted the town's forty new automobiles and every-thing they symbolized, and they clearly understood how their bread was buttered. "The peculiar sulphur taste of the smelter fumes was everywhere noticeable," the *Courier-Free Press* sang, "and the people of Shasta County instead of being oth-erwise are glad of the fact that once more the air is laden with smoke from the smelters, for it reminds them of the palmy days of old Keswick which added to the county's prosperity."[2]

Redding's vision of prosperity presumably excluded the wildfires that gradually were licking up the fume-killed wood-lands on all sides of the city. The spring of 1908 had been un-commonly dry and hot and had ushered in an especially bad fire season. At the end of May fires burning north and east of Kennett threatened to descend on the smelter town itself, and a considerable part of Mammoth's crew had to be turned out to set backfires and quelch flare-ups. In July there was a big conflagration in the brush and stumps between Keswick and Redding, and the leaping flames kept people in both towns entertained for several nights. In August several home-steads and considerable timber were lost when a five-mile swath of country burned east of Redding. Smaller brush fires also swept ranches south and west of the city that month.[3]

And there were grave indications that smelter smoke was undermining more than just the vegetable landscape. In dark parallel, the floating poisons that made century-old trees blanch and die in a year seemed to be exercising a pernicious influence on human well-being too. In the spring of 1908 the death rate from respiratory complaints in Kennett ran so

---

[2] Ibid., October 21, 24, 1908. See also Martin, "The Balaklala Mine and Smelter, Cal-ifornia," 1163–66

[3] *Redding Courier Free-Press*, May 26, July 21, August 1–2, 11, 1908.

high it spawned rumors that bubonic plague had broken out there, attracting the attention of investigators from the state board of health. Mammoth's resident manager denounced the plague report as "the most incredible exaggeration of any of the stories that have got into circulation concerning the health of our community." The company doctor blamed the prevalence of throat and lung infections on the mephitic rabble of tramps who had flocked to Kennett the previous fall in a vain hope for jobs, then tumbled into squalid cribs for the winter.[4]

The good doctor's unguarded diagnosis of the situation betrayed what must have been an exceptional degree of anxiety. Ordinarily the smelter's friends and servants missed no occasion to tout Kennett as a model company town in every respect, a community of not only glowing health but also "churches, progressive businessmen, fine homes and families." A cursory flip through newspapers of the period suggests it was really about as tough and trouble-breeding a place as old Keswick ever was, with the same tawdry tales of broken-down grifters, lewd women, crazy stabbing frays, and blind pig raids cropping up with about the same frequency. Its "Little Italy" section alone supported eight wide-open grog joints. Many years later a former Kennett lad shared some of his tender boyhood memories of the community:

> Right near there on the way up the hill there were a bunch of whorehouses and some one hundred women. It was the biggest operation like this in California! I asked Dad who those women washing clothes in the creek were and he said, "Well—you'll know some day—those are bad women."

---

[4] *Redding Searchlight*, March 29, 31, 1908. The bubonic plague report at Kennett was not so far-fetched as it may sound: health authorities at the time were contending with genuine outbreaks in the city of San Francisco and various counties east and north of San Francisco Bay; see California Board of Health, *Report for 1906–1908* (Sacramento: State Printer, 1908), 15–18. On the adverse health effects of sulfur dioxide, see Robert Frank, "Acute and Chronic Respiratory Effects of Exposure to Inhaled Toxic Agents," in Merchant, *Occupational Respiratory Diseases*, 599–602.

There were many deaths at the mine and they used to lay them out in the assay house, next to the post office. Most of them were caused by blasting or cave-ins. We kids used to sneak in there to look at them sometimes—it was very scary! . . .

At the mine there was no store of any kind except notions and candy, no liquor. But even without liquor we had a lot of fights among the foreigners. We kids used to watch them chew each others' ears off![5]

It was, however, for the sake of private property, not public health or morals, that the next phase of the smoke war would be fought, as surrounding farmers and ranchers recognized the need to pick up a big stick to protect their equities. The county's fruit growers had enjoyed two good years after the curtailment of operations at Keswick, but the two additional furnaces and double-high smokestack that had been erected at the Kennett smelter the previous winter already were showing their evil effects. The 1908 prune harvest was nothing short of disastrous, and on many ranches what little there was of a crop was merely shaken down for the hogs. Two four-hundred-ton blast furnaces at the new Coram smelter began adding their toxic burden to the atmosphere later that fall.[6]

In the spring of 1909 the Balaklala smelter got its third big blast furnace in operation and also blew in a reverberatory furnace and two of its four McDougall roasters. The Mammoth smelter had four of its five blast furnaces running full capacity, and much of the ore being put through reportedly was high-arsenic stuff brought in from the Nevada mines of its parent company. Sulfur dioxide emissions from the two plants reached peak levels that season, and although the prune growers around Anderson got a lucky harvest, in Happy Valley and elsewhere the burning of vegetation and loss of crops was widespread and severe. By summer the situation was reaching the

[5] Lowden, "Life at the Mammoth Mine, 1907–1918," 37. *Covered Wagon* is the annual publication of the Shasta Historical Society.

[6] *Redding Searchlight*, September 3, October 21, December 17, 1908.

Two views of the so-called Butter's Dam, up Big Backbone Creek some five miles north of Kennett. It would serve as the main water reservoir for Mammoth Copper's new town and smelter at Kennett. *Top:* ca. 1904, photographer unknown. Image 307,584. *Bottom:* From 1939, showing total destruction of surrounding forest by smelter fumes, 1905–19, with slow recovery over next twenty years. Photograph by René Bollaert. Image 392,138. Images from Photographs and Research Data, Pacific Southwest Forest and Range Experiment Station, U.S. Forest Service, Federal Records Center, San Bruno, California.

boiling point. "This part of California is literally scorched," a Redding farmer complained to the U.S. attorney general's office. "It looks as if a fire had swept over it, destroying all kinds of vegetation." He told of fruit and alfalfa ranches properly worth $20,000 or more that had lost half their crops and perhaps all their market value because of the deadly fumes.[7]

In an effort to head off the rising storm, agents of the two companies had been making the rounds of the farming districts, interviewing proprietors and suggesting deals in the form of so-called smoke easements, whereby the farmer would sign articles relinquishing his future right of action in exchange for regular damage payments on an agreed-upon schedule. Fifty to a hundred dollars down and one to two hundred dollars a year was rumored to be the standard offer. Happy Valley farmers gathered at the Olinda schoolhouse on the evening of August 7, 1909, to discuss their losses and compare notes on the propositions the companies were offering. They concluded that as long as injuries continued on the present scale they never could accept any indemnity less than the full value of their properties. A resolution passed by the meeting warned individuals against signing questionnaires or any other papers that might be circulated by the companies, and suggested formation of a permanent countywide league for the purpose of effecting "such united action as shall in some way give us relief and secure to us our homes for which we have given the best part of our lives."[8]

No doubt the embattled farmers would have signed on to the sentiments expressed in a brief filed by the State Department in an unrelated smelter-smoke case on the U.S.-Canada border twenty years later:

---

[7] Lambeth E. Gibson to Department of Agriculture, August 9, 1909, and L. E. Gibson to Wade H. Ellis, September 8, 1909, in DOJ 144276; *Engineering and Mining Journal* 88 (1909), 279.

[8] *Redding Searchlight*, August 12, 1909; *Red Bluff Daily News*, August 11, 17, 19, 20, 1909; *Engineering and Mining Journal* 87 (1909), 467.

Looking across completely barren mountainsides above Kennett, 1922, just three years after Mammoth smelter ceased operation. Photograph by E. N. Munns. Image 175,314, Photographs and Research Data, Pacific Southwest Forest and Range Experiment Station, U.S. Forest Service, Federal Records Center, San Bruno, California.

The farmers desire to operate their farms without trespass or interference. They do not desire to labor under the burden of having their crops injured, even though some compensation may be made therefor; nor do they desire to face a future holding unknown factors such as the possibility of fatal crop injuries, inadequate compensation, and prolonged negotiations. They desire to pursue their duties free from hindrances except those arising naturally from conditions subsisting in their vicinity, and they have a right to do so. Facing the menace of these fumes, they are uncertain whether when they sow they shall reap. They are subject to mental turmoil and interference with home and community life. They are under the necessity continuously to reckon with sulphur dioxide. . . . Is

this to continue indefinitely? How are these people to show what
their losses actually are day after day and year after year? How can
the damages resulting from the loss of credit and the destruction of
the market value of their property be determined? . . . By what theory of law, by what standard of morals can these conditions be permitted to continue?[9]

The Anderson Chamber of Commerce sponsored a mass
meeting on the smelter-smoke question on the evening of
August 20, 1909, filling the town's Odd Fellows' Hall with
determined farmers and ranchers from all over the county,
along with a worried delegation of businessmen from Redding who wanted to register their opposition to "any radical
or ill-advised move that will harm the general prosperity."
Many of the farmers insisted that closing the smelters
peremptorily and permanently was the only real solution, but
the tentative policy adopted by the majority was less drastic.
From the local chapters that had sprung up around the
county over the previous two weeks a consolidated organization was created, christened the Shasta County Farmers'
Protective Association. An executive committee was ap-
pointed to work out an appropriate strategy and open an official dialogue with the management of the smelters.[10]

Initial contacts were not encouraging. The resident manager at the Mammoth smelter assured the farmers that his
company was anxious to minimize damage, but he had no
authority to say anything specific until the matter had been
referred to the eastern offices. No promises were extracted
from Balaklala's manager, either. The farmers interpreted the
companies' attitude as evasive. A packed meeting the following Saturday passed a firm resolution demanding that the
smoke and fumes nuisance cease and that the companies give
official word within thirty days of what they proposed to do

[9] Metzger, *Trail Smelter Reference*, 96–97. See also Wirth, *Smelter Smoke in North America*, 9–44.
[10] *Redding Searchlight*, August 15, 20, 1909; *Redding Courier-Free Press*, August 21, 1909.

about it. "The question is one for calm, deliberate action," the *Redding Courier-Free Press* squeaked, "not for radical, almost anarchistic, treatment."[11]

The next meeting was crowded and clamorous, "a scene of wild confusion," according to one account. It was addressed by Mammoth's attorney, Alfred Sutro, who had come from San Francisco in an attempt to beg more time, at least till November, to formulate an official response. The supercilious lawyer struck a sour note with seething ranchers who already were convinced his company was bent on playing for time indefinitely. At one point he reportedly told his hecklers they were no better than "a flock of cackling geese," unable to comprehend the smoke problem in its whole complexity. "He came nearly being mobbed." But the farmers recognized that for the time being they were helpless, their organization being still without any formal standing—no charter, no officers, no funds. At a subsequent meeting they drew up an official list of members and elected an executive committee, choosing as president McCoy Fitzgerald, a well-heeled Clear Creek rancher who happened to hold a law degree from Harvard. Soon afterward the protective association engaged the services of a well-known Redding attorney, T. W. H. Shanahan. Shanahan was finishing his fifth term in the state assembly, where he had compiled a solid record as a Populist/Democrat. As chair of the assembly judiciary committee he had been instrumental in securing the Australian ballot in California elections; he also had been a strong voice for the initiative, referendum, and recall, as well as for Asiatic exclusion, free school textbooks, railroad reassessment, and other progressive causes. His family's own-

---

[11] *Redding Courier-Free Press*, August 26, 30, 1909. My cross-check of the founding membership of the Shasta County Farmers' Protective Association with the 1912 county register of voters turned up sixty-five Republicans, among them Charles Paige, and forty-nine Democrats, among them McCoy Fitzgerald. Another ten were Socialists, two were Progressives, and three were undeclared. This hardly profiles a "radical" or "anarchistic" movement.

ership of a large prune orchard in Anderson Valley made him
an especially dependable selection in the farmers' eyes.[12]

The companies got the extra time they wanted and both
sides set about fortifying their positions during the period of
truce. The farmers' protective association, whose compiled
membership roll showed 205 names representing title to over
thirty thousand acres of land, determined to assess dues
equivalent to 25 percent of the county property taxes paid by
each member. This was a stiff levy indeed in recessionary
times, but the ranchers grimly looked ahead to a costly, pro-
tracted, and malefic struggle despite the companies' profes-
sions of good faith. It was known that Balaklala already had
put a "botanical expert" in the field, the notorious Dr. J. W.
Blankenship, whose suborned testimony had helped Amalgamated Copper defeat the smoke suit brought against it by
the farmers of Deerlodge Valley, Montana, in a federal case
decided just that January. That bruising, four-year contest
had cost the Deerlodge farmers $200,000 and brought many
of them to the brink of bankruptcy. Amalgamated reportedly
had spent $600,000 to discredit their claims, bringing up the
slickest legal and scientific talent that money could buy.[13]

The industry also was tuning up its propaganda organs,
suggesting a defense along the lines of the same "higher principles of equity" that had been successfully invoked by the
Mountain Copper Company in its recent struggle with the
U.S. government. "It is physically possible to abate the
smelter-fume difficulty, but it has not yet proven economically possible to do it," San Francisco's *Mining and Scientific
Press* editorialized. "There is a heavy burden of proof de-
volving on the Shasta farmers to show that the smelters can

[12] *Redding Searchlight*, September 5, 1909; *Redding Courier-Free Press*, September 6,
1909. See also "Susan Walker FitzGerald Papers: Description of Collection," Special Collections Department, Bryn Mawr College Library, Bryn Mawr, Penn.
[13] *Redding Searchlight*, September 12, 16, 1909. See also MacMillan, *Smoke Wars*, 101–
43; Murphy, *The Comical History of Montana*, 201–21.

obey their mandate without financial ruin." The journal argued for a "rational utilitarianism" that would respect the larger working population as well as the preponderant financial interest dependent on the smelters. "This is not a world of sentiment, but a world to live in, and all cannot be happy in it at the same time. . . . The greatest justice for the greatest number has always determined the ultimate course of society, individualistic rights to the contrary notwithstanding." The present difficulty could be smoothed out easily enough with cash indemnities to the farmers, the journal counseled—so long as the rubes did not try to "over-reach and demand damages in such sums as might give rise to suspicion of blackmail." A Chicago journal agreed that in any event the farmers must not be allowed to "maliciously injure one of the most important of industries."[14]

But as a matter of fact the Shasta smelters could no longer count on Judge Ross's balance-of-injury logic in the Mountain Copper case as solid precedent. It had been set back temporarily by a decision handed down by the Eighth U.S. Circuit Court of Appeals at Minneapolis in 1907. In that contest, 409 farmers owning some nine thousand acres of land in Utah's Salt Lake Valley obtained a permanent injunction against four big smelters situated at the south end of the valley. "They are," the Salt Lake farmers complained of the smelters, "fast converting a valley thickly populated, prolific in its fertility . . . into one of discomfort, desolation, and death." The complainants told how valuable fruit orchards had been blighted by the sulfur, lead, and arsenic fumes; how grain and alfalfa crops were bleached and burned, livestock and honey bees poisoned and killed, by the same.[15]

The Utah smelting companies replied that all injuries

[14] "Smelter Fume and Equity," Mining and Scientific Press 99 (1909), 306–307; "The California Farmer-Smelter War," Mining World 31 (1909), 587.

[15] "Brief of Argument for James Godfrey, et al., Appellees," 2–8, in CCA 2549. See also Lamborn and Peterson, "The Substance of the Land," 308–25.

were grossly overstated, but even if persons in the immediate
vicinity suffered in their property or comfort the courts still
should compel them to "yield to the public good." The four
smelters were generating millions for their investors and for
the general public, and to break them up by court decree
would be nothing less than "an abuse of power." A stop-work
injunction would result in "the destruction of great property
values, the throwing of many men out of employment, with
the attending hardships to themselves and families, and great
injury to the public at large and to the State."[16]

To which the farmers indignantly answered:

> We earnestly insist that the destruction of the farms, homes, and
> property of the thousands of people inhabiting Salt Lake Valley, to-
> gether with the injury to their health, conclusively demonstrates
> that the "balance of injury" greatly preponderates upon the side of
> the complainants. We are amazed that there can be any question
> upon this point. . . . The area of devastation and destruction is con-
> stantly increasing, so that, as stated, but a few years will result in the
> complete ruin of the agricultural lands of a large and fertile valley.
> This would mean that thousands of families would be compelled to
> abandon their homes and seek employment elsewhere. It would
> mean that hundreds of thousands of dollars of agricultural products
> produced annually would be lost. We submit that measured by the
> standard of dollars and cents, which is the only one these tyrannous
> and powerful corporations invoke, the loss to the State and the na-
> tion would be much greater if the injunction be denied and the
> predatory course of these corporations legalized.[17]

That predatory course, the Utah farmers insisted, involved
not just the physical destruction of their property but the
voiding of their common-law and constitutional rights as
well. And if legitimized by a federal court it would mean
nothing less than "the enthronement of the doctrine that
Capital and Power are supreme, and that governments and

---

[16] "Brief for United States Smelting Company," 56, in CCA 2549.
[17] "Brief for Godfrey et al.," 31, in CCA 2549.

courts are constituted to aid in their inviolability and to restrain the impious hands of the multitude whom they may
oppress."[18]

The Utah farmers' petition for an injunction was granted
by the district court and upheld by the circuit court of appeals. The federal judges concluded that injuries to health
and property wrought by the smelters were indeed substantial, continuous, cumulative, and incapable of adequate
measurement and reparation. "And when the acts of the defendants produce this result, as is clearly shown by the record
in this case, the court is bound to protect such individual
rights." The companies' balance-of-injury argument was
brushed aside completely. "The parties to this suit, upon both
sides, have important and very valuable interests affected by
the decree, and it would indeed be difficult to say which side
would suffer the greater injury," wrote Judge John Riner of
Wyoming. "However that may be, we do not think the fact
that an actual injury resulting from the violation of a right is
small, and the interest to be affected by an injunction is
large, should weigh against the interposition of preventive
power in equity, when it is clear that on one hand a right is
violated and on the other a wrong committed."[19]

One of the defendant smelters in the Utah case was a subsidiary of United States Smelting, Refining, and Mining of
Boston, Mammoth's parent company. In August 1909, about
the time affairs in Shasta County were coming to a head, the
company had secured court approval of a modification of the
1907 injunction that allowed it to resume full-scale operation after installing a new system of fume control. The mod-
ified decree provided that all free acids be removed from the
smoke by addition of neutralizing chemicals, that all dust and

---

[18] Ibid., 36.
[19] "American Smelting and Refining Co., et al., v. Godfrey, et al.," *Federal Reporter* 158
(1908), 229–34.

fume particles be removed by filtration through a baghouse, and that the sulfur dioxide content of the escaping gases be reduced to below 0.75 percent by dilution with fresh air. There would be plenty of complaints about this arrangement later on, but temporarily it gave satisfaction, and the press gave due publicity to the era of good feeling supposedly dawning in the Salt Lake Valley. Mammoth's top officials came west in October to promote the so-called Utah Decree as a model for resolving the analogous impasse in Shasta County. A preliminary agreement was drawn up along those lines by the farmers' attorney and accepted unanimously by a full meeting of the protective association in November 1909. Shanahan was authorized to meet with Mammoth's legal staff to hammer out details of a "friendly suit" that would be entered in federal court to make the contract fully binding. Mammoth immediately had a construction crew begin excavations on the hill behind the Kennett plant.[20]

Conferences, explanations, and pleas for more time continued all winter and into the spring. By February 1910, a final version of the agreement with Mammoth was ready to submit to the membership of the farmers' protective association, after being reviewed and endorsed by the executive committee, Assemblyman Shanahan, and Hiram Johnson, a progressive San Francisco attorney who was stumping the northern part of the state as the Republican Party's probable candidate in the upcoming gubernatorial election. The agreement's ratification was moved, seconded, and carried without a dissenting vote. "The assembly burst into loud applause." By April the foundation for the baghouse was laid and work on the superstructure was beginning.

The Balaklala company also was coming to terms, but more slowly. In April the company accepted the general pro-

---

[20] *Redding Courier-Free Press*, October 22–23, November 15, 1909.

visions of the Utah Decree but submitted plans to substitute an electrical precipitation plant in place of the baghouse method for clearing its smoke. The effectiveness of the so-called Cottrell process was not so well demonstrated but promised the advantages of much lower first cost and greater quickness and compactness of installation. The farmers, more concerned with results than methods anyhow, were persuaded of the proposal's workability and approved it the following month. Work on the plant began right away. The Mammoth and Balaklala companies both pledged to have their smoke control apparatuses in commission by July 1. In consenting to this the farmers showed laudable patience indeed, for it was already evident that the Shasta fruit crop was again going to be very meager. All spring, while negotiations dragged along, smelting had continued unabated, Balaklala every day treating over eight hundred tons of ore averaging 34 percent sulfur, and Mammoth some eleven hundred tons running 40 percent. This meant that over fourteen hundred tons of sulfur dioxide were being diffused over the region daily, almost twice the quantity given off by the Keswick plant during its heyday.[21]

At the end of June 1910, the representatives of Mammoth and the farmers gathered in San Francisco to present their agreement for approval by the U.S. district court. C. D. Sprague, the company engineer who had designed the original baghouse in Utah, assured Judge William Morrow that the furnace smoke would be freed of all deleterious elements except the sulfur dioxide, which would be released in such weak concentrations as to be "perfectly harmless." He said the baghouse had been in operation in Utah for more than

---

[21] Ibid., November 1, 5, 1909; February 11, 18, 24, March 10, April 4, 11, 25, May 12, 16, 1910; *Redding Searchlight*, February 24, March 4, 1910; *Engineering and Mining Journal* 89 (1910), 839. See also Cottrell, "The Electrical Precipitation of Suspended Particles," 542–50; Olin, *California's Prodigal Sons*, 22–26.

a year with no complaints from surrounding farmers, even
though a large and valuable acreage of grain, alfalfa, and fruit
land was in the vicinity. General Manager George Metcalfe
would not say there had been no complaints in Utah, only
that his company had removed all good cause for complaint.
He did positively state that there would be no further damage to vegetation in Shasta County once the baghouse was
up, pointing out that his company was staking "something
over $200,000" on its success. Speaking for the farmers,
Shanahan declared that he had found nothing to contradict
the claims made for the proposal and that he was satisfied
the decree "will constitute an adequate remedy for the condition of affairs that exists in our country at the present mo-
ment." The instrument included provisions that allowed the
farmers to inspect the plant from time to time for compli-
ance, and also reserved their individual right to put in claims
for damages. At the same time it bound them not to initiate
any other actions for injunction against the smelter, indi-
vidually or collectively. A general clause was inserted that
the smoke would be so discharged and diffused as not to injure crops, trees, or livestock, or cause the complainants or
their families any harm or discomfort. "It seems to me to be
a pretty safe decree," remarked Judge Morrow.[22]

The decree entered with the court that day stipulated first
of all that the smoke be completely freed of all sulfur trioxide and sulfuric acid—both corrosive compounds, bad
enough in their own way, but really only minor factors in the
general destruction of crops and vegetation. In Utah special
measures had to be provided to thus "neutralize" the smoke,
but company chemists were confident that the high natural
zinc oxide content of Mammoth's ore would secure the desired result here without additional treatment. The decree

[22] "Reporter's Transcript, Friday, June 24th, 1910," in NDC 15122.

also required that all fine solids—flue dust, metallic oxides, and mineral salts—be strained out of the smoke by passing it through a baghouse. When the Mammoth baghouse was finally up and running it was found to be catching around fifteen tons of particles a day. Assays showed that most of this dust was zinc sulfate, which was of little consequence one way or the other, although alarming percentages of lead and arsenic also were revealed. The baghouse undoubtedly was a good thing for human and animal life in the vicinity, but here again conditions for plant life in the region would not have been improved very much by its operation. Concerning sulfur dioxide, the really destructive component of the smoke, the decree mandated no reduction at all in absolute volume but only required that its concentration in the exit gases be kept below 0.75 percent. This was to be achieved simply by blowing in outside air with a set of huge fans. Why the stipulated threshold was deemed adequate in the first place is not clear: 0.75 percent was three times the sulfur dioxide concentration allowed under recent amendments to the Alkali Act which governed industrial smoke emissions in Great Britain, and three thousand times what contemporary plant pathologists knew could stunt and kill growing vegetation. The industry, in any case, was pleased with the bargain. "It is the way of peace, economy, and good will," cooed the *Mining and Scientific Press*.[23]

The baghouse of which so much was expected was a rather

---

[23] "Smelter Fume Compromise," *Mining and Scientific Press* 100 (1910), 383; Topper, "Copper Smelting at the Kennett Plant, California," 337–39; Nevius, "Shasta County Smelter-Fume Problems," 374–77. Compare Davenport, King, Schlesinger, and Biswas, *Extractive Metallurgy of Copper*, 218; see also Ashby and Anderson, *The Politics of Clean Air*, 77–81. The optimism and good cheer stimulated by the farmer-smelter agreement was enough to lift Shanahan into the state senate in elections that fall, but the nettles of strife were hardly eradicated. McCoy Fitzgerald's bid for county district attorney was knocked down decisively by the votes of Redding, Kennett, and Coram: see *Redding Courier-Free Press*, November 19, 1910.

remarkable piece of engineering and it merits a more detailed description. The old smokestack at the Kennett plant was entirely blocked off and the fumes and gases redirected through a set of big steel flues to a "fanhouse" two hundred feet up the hill. At this station two huge paddlewheel fans whirled in fresh air to cool and dilute the smoke. From there the smoke was driven another two hundred feet through a complex of cooling pipes leading up to the baghouse. By now the furnace smoke had been mixed about four-to-one with outside air and its temperature had been brought down from over 500°F to less than 200°F. Through a distributing chamber controlled with giant flap valves the smoke was delivered into the baghouse proper. This was a great barn-like structure, divided into five bays, each of which contained six hundred bags suspended mouth downward from shaker rods. These "bags" in fact were gargantuan wool socks, thirty-four feet long and eighteen inches in diameter. The mouth of each bag fit over a circular opening in the floor through which the draft forced its way upward. The bags ballooned with smoke, the gases oozing through while the solid particles caught in the wool meshes. When the bags in one bay began to clog, that chamber was shut off and the bags were shaken clean, the dust dropping into brick hoppers below the floor.[24]

The first smoke was turned into the Mammoth baghouse on July 5 1910, the glad tidings sharing headlines in Redding's afternoon paper with the sensational news of the Jack Johnson-Jim Jeffries fight in Reno the day before. It took a few days to adjust the draft properly, but when that was done the facility was working "like a dream," according to optimists. "Smelter smoke is from this time on a reminiscence," the *Courier-Free Press* cheered. "Smelter smoke is ancient history." But the cooling system failed to live up to calcula-

---

[24] Hofman, *Metallurgy of Copper*, 228–29; Rice, "Handling Copper Smeltery Gases," 614–17.

tions, and before long it was seen that the hot exhaust of four big blast furnaces was scorching and eroding the wool bags. Two of the furnaces had to be shut down and 165 men were laid off at the mine and smelter. It was hoped that a third furnace perhaps could be run in the cold of winter, but for the plant to get back to full capacity a major remodeling would have to be undertaken. Company engineers began drafting plans for an enlargement of the flues and installation of a new bank of cooling pipes.[25]

Soon after the Mammoth baghouse went into commission, representatives of the Balaklala company appeared before Judge Morrow in San Francisco to finalize their smoke control agreement with the farmers. Professor F. G. Cottrell of Berkeley, inventor of the electrical precipitation apparatus being installed at Coram, explained the scheme to the court and assured that it would effectively clear the smoke of arsenic and other solid particles and to that extent would "reduce the quantity of deleterious matter in general." But he admitted that it would not eliminate the sulfur dioxide, that no known contrivance would: "We do not make any claim that it will affect the sulphur dioxide any more than the baghouse will affect it. It is simply to parallel the action of the baghouse. We claim no more or less for its action than that of the baghouse." General Manager R. T. White emphasized that Balaklala was only following what had been stipulated in the Mammoth decree. He promised that the Coram smelter would have its precipitation plant in by October 1910, acknowledging that any interim operation would be at the farmers' sufferance. If there were any complaints of substantial damage the smelter would be shut down "without the necessity of being dragged into court. We want to get along harmoniously if we can." Shanahan, in turn, said the

----

[25] *Redding Courier-Free Press*, July 5, 6, 23, 1910.

farmers did not intend to be antagonistic or unfair, but warned that they would not tolerate anything "of a character that would seem to involve ruin."[26]

The understanding that was supposed to bridge the three months till October failed to hold up three weeks. No sooner had the decree been filed than farmers were complaining about fresh smoke damage and wondering why the company should not be forced to dabble at its own expense. Balaklala tried to placate them by cutting back to only one furnace running just three hundred tons of ore a day. There were several more long conferences at Coram, Redding, and San Francisco, and the usual pleas for leniency and compromise. The question finally was referred to the general membership of the farmers' protective association at the end of July 1910. Angry ranchers stood up to accuse the company of malingering and were "loudly cheered." With only two dissenting votes the meeting decided to order the smelter to shut down if it could not comply strictly and promptly with the terms of the agreement. Balaklala's lawyer remarked that the company obviously had "put its head in the lion's mouth" by signing the decree, but said it would abide by the association's dictate and close within thirty days. Properly, it had no choice.[27]

It was said that one thousand men were thrown out of work by the shutdown of the Balaklala smelter and the slowdown at Mammoth. A disgusted Coram merchant remarked that if the community had been put to this inconvenience by labor troubles the whole state militia would have been called out. But if the mercantile element was bitter about the state of affairs, the county's farmers were more so. The Anderson prune crop in 1910 was down an estimated 75 percent while pears were off at least 50 percent, and the situation was only

---

[26] "Reporter's Transcript, Friday, July 8th, 1910," in NDC 15123.

[27] *Redding Courier-Free Press*, July 16, 21–23, 25, 30, 1910; *Redding Searchlight*, July 22–24, 26, 1910.

partially compensated by unusually high fruit prices. A free-thinking Redding citizen wondered a little about the smelters' favorite public-relations line, "the greatest good for the greatest number." He contrasted the future promised by local horticulturists, one of "steady abundance" and "ever-renewing life," with the "sudden vigor followed by decay and death" represented by nonresident investors who would exploit the hills according to their own transient purposes, leaving behind "exhausted holes in the ground" and "desolate, cheerless wastes." The emergence of just such a wasteland was becoming increasingly evident to local people. The summer of 1910 was a bad one for wildfires all over the West, and the dried-out woodlands of the Shasta County smoke belt proved to be especially liable. At the close of July a big fire swept the mountains between Keswick and Coram; a few weeks later a conflagration above Happy Valley destroyed many of the flumes of the local irrigation company. Leaders of the farmers' protective association warned that this sort of thing was going to be a perennial problem given the abundance of desiccated brush in the region.[28]

Various outside interests also were finding cause for concern and grounds for action. A San Francisco capitalist with extensive riparian holdings above Kennett filed a big damage suit against Mammoth in July 1910, saying the smelter had "poisoned, crippled, and injured" the timber on more than five thousand acres of his land. And that fall it was disclosed that the Southern Pacific Railroad Company had agreed to contribute $1,135 toward the expenses of the Shasta County Farmers' Protective Association, approximately 20 percent of the latter's outlay on legal bills that year. Although Kennett and Coram were said to be the best paying stations in the state north of Sacramento, the landslides and washouts

---

[28] *Redding Courier-Free Press*, April 2, July 29, August 17, 1910; *Redding Searchlight*, July 28, November 18, 1910.

that occurred in the denuded canyon with almost every
storm had made that section of line the most costly to main-
tain in the railroad's whole network, and the company had
been put to great expense constructing hundreds of new
ditches and culverts in an effort to protect its roadbed. The
Southern Pacific also happened to be one of the area's biggest
landowners and therefore had a direct proprietary interest in
seeing the fumes controlled. Even the smoke-dependent
communities of Kennett and Coram were acknowledging
some serious embarrassments from the devastation of local
watersheds. Earlier that year they had lobbied for a new
county main road up the canyon, because the old highway
had become so badly washed and eroded. "This is a condition
that cannot be helped around any smelter." It also was expected that the new road would make accessible some surviving patches of native timber and help relieve the gnawing
fuel wood scarcity in the smelter towns. "Wood is a necessity,
like the food we eat, and must be had at any cost."[29]

Uncle Sam was not unconscious of the situation. At one
point the U.S. Department of Justice contemplated bringing
suits for injunction against the two smelters, but later decided to postpone action and eventually compromised its
claim. The government was bound to be rather circumspect
about mixing it up again with the industry, so soon after its
enervating struggle with the Mountain Copper Company. It
probably was too late to save anything of consequence, any-
way. A Forest Service man spent several days in August 1910
investigating conditions around Kennett and Coram. He
found that total or near-total destruction of vegetation al-

---

[29] *Redding Searchlight*, January 12, 14, 1910; *Redding Courier-Free Press*, July 23, October 30, 1910. See also, Orsi, *Sunset Limited*, 394–95. It seems the archives of the now-de-
funct railroad company have been scattered or lost since Orsi's 1980s research: Richard J.
Orsi (California State University–East Bay, Hayward, Calif.) to Khaled J. Bloom, August
9, 2004 (author's files).

ready extended all along the lower canyon of the Sacramento, from north of Kennett south almost to Redding. Dry, brown leaves and needles clung to dying shrubs and trees over many square miles surrounding the barren gorge, and the beginnings of serious soil erosion already were apparent. He correctly perceived that neither the baghouse nor the Cottrell apparatus would eliminate any of the sulfur dioxide and so would do nothing at all to relieve the killing of vegetation, "except to the slight extent which the deposition of solid particles on the foliage may have influenced it." In effect, neither device would serve to do anything but "make the fumes colorless." He called the situation "a great pity."[30]

At the end of September 1910, Balaklala reassembled its crew and restarted operations at the Coram smelter. Hot smoke rising off the furnaces was turned through a brick flue leading straight into the new Cottrell condensation plant, where a direct current of thirty thousand volts was distributed through a cross section of six thousand discharge electrodes. Dust and fume particles became positively charged passing through this field and precipitated electrostatically onto five thousand ten-foot strips of boiler plate hanging from crossbars. Like the baghouse, the Cottrell plant was partitioned into five chambers, each of which could be closed off as necessary so the collecting electrodes could be rattled clean, the dust falling down into hoppers whence it was removed by screw conveyors. Precooling of the smoke was not necessary under this system, but two enormous fans were provided at the base of the smokestack to suck in fresh air and keep the sulfur dioxide concentration below the stipulated maximum of 0.75 percent.[31]

---

[30] J. D. Coffman to R. F. Hammatt, September 26, 1910, in FS RCF.
[31] *Redding Courier-Free Press*, August 20, September 8, 24, 26, 28, 1910; Hofman, *Metallurgy of Copper*, 229–31; Martin, "The Balaklala Smelter and Cottrell Fume Controller," 337–39. See also LeCain, "The Limits of 'Eco-Efficiency,'" 336–51.

It was apparent right away that the Cottrell device was not operating so smoothly as the blueprints had promised. Voltage fluctuated, electrodes clogged, and clouds of visible smoke were still rising from the stack. The company struggled to improve performance by rearranging the flues and dampers, putting in new transformers, and changing the electrodes. One unlucky engineer was electrocuted when he tripped over a high-tension wire during a test. At the end of October 1910, a committee of farmers visited Coram and listened to the manager's explanations. They came away willing to give the smelter a little more time: "You may say for us that there is no disposition on our part to harass the Balaklala." But after a few weeks it began to look as though toleration was no longer a virtue. Not only was Balaklala back to running full capacity, but the Mammoth smelter had taken advantage of the cooler weather to blow in a third furnace, and many farmers were noting serious injury to crops and vegetation on their places. Another ultimatum from the protective association forced Balaklala to shut down for two weeks in December. The smelter made a few more alterations and adjustments, then started up again at the end of the month with one furnace. The company proclaimed that its Cottrell condenser now was working better than expected or required, and it announced plans to blow in its other two furnaces right after the new year. "I fail to see where any improvements could be made," General Manager White was quoted as saying.[32]

The autumn of 1910 had been unusually long and dry, and the streets in Redding were being sprinkled to lay the dust as late as Christmas. Another of those brush fires that gradually were reducing the country north of town to a state of lunar barrenness was running over the hills between Coram

---

[32] *Redding Courier-Free Press*, November 1, December 3, 12–13, 28, 1910; *Redding Searchlight*, October 26, 30, December 2, 4, 13–14, 17, 1910.

and Kennett, and the pall of acrid smoke lay heavy in the still air. "Clouds of smoke hanging against the northern hills are declared by the sensitive farmers to be smelter smoke." Another grievance committee went up to Coram. The company's attorneys attempted to curb ill feeling and buy time by paying off a couple of dozen outstanding damage claims, but farmer dissatisfaction still festered. The price of copper was a little stronger by now and the company's resistance was stiffening. It not only declined to shut down but went ahead and started its other furnaces. In January 1911, the Shasta County Farmers' Protective Association served Balaklala with another written notice, which brought in reply a note to the effect that the company believed it was substantially conforming to the decree. This was taken to be a polite but firm message that the smelter had no intention of abridging its operations and would fight in the courts if necessary to keep running full swing.[33]

A general meeting of the protective association at Anderson early the next month drew a crowd of over four hundred intensely frustrated ranchers. Fruit trees were about to blossom, and the growing season was at hand. Recognizing that they lacked the hard data necessary to substantiate their accusations, the farmers approved the hiring of professional chemists and resolved to bring suit immediately if the investigation confirmed that Balaklala was in violation of the previous year's agreement. It was going to take several weeks to arrange the tests, and Shanahan warned that it probably would take at least another month after that to get their application up before a federal judge for consideration.[34]

The chemical tests were conducted in March and April 1911, and the results were presented in May. Farmers who

---

[33] *Redding Courier-Free Press*, December 27, 29, 1910; *Redding Searchlight*, December 31, 1910, January 3, 6, 29, 1911.

[34] *Redding Courier-Free Press*, February 4, 1911.

were doleful about another miserable fruit set must have
been cheered a bit by the findings, which showed that Balaklala had failed on all counts to comply with the 1910
smoke decree. A total of forty-four tests had been made at
reasonable intervals, each consisting of two determinations:
one sample drawn from the mouth of the flue before the
smoke had passed through the Cottrell apparatus, the other
taken at the base of the stack after the smoke had gone
through the precipitator and been diluted with air. Each and
every test showed that considerable quantities of dust and
appreciable amounts of sulfuric acid were passing out into
the atmosphere. The clearance of mist and particles from the
smoke stream averaged only 72 percent and occasionally fell
as low as 20 percent. Sulfur dioxide exceeded 0.75 percent in
eight of the forty-four tests.[35]

The farmers submitted the report and two dozen supporting affidavits to Judge Morrow in San Francisco, who cited
Balaklala to appear in July and show cause why it should not
be punished for contempt. The farmers fully expected a battle royal. The company had been accused of shifty dealing
all along and was believed to have assembled a trove of dishonest counterevidence to undercut the farmers' prima facie
showing. But when the day of the hearing arrived the company put up no resistance at all, and its lawyer, Curtis Lindley, struck an apologetic attitude. He admitted that the
company had set Professor Blankenship to work that spring
in an effort to show that complaints of damage to crops and
other property were largely "sentimental" and that the
smelter was "being made scapegoat." Lindley explained: "We
were strongly impressed with the idea that a psychological
condition existed in that section of the country, in what we
might call the smoke zone, and that the good people up there

[35] McCoy Fitzgerald affidavit, May 25, 1911, and John S. Burd affidavit, May 25, 1911, in NDC 15123.

engaged in the farming industry were somewhat disposed to charge against the Balaklala injuries which were caused by other than smelter smoke." But there had been, he suavely acknowledged, "later occurrences" and "later revelations" that forced the company to concede that "the claims of those gentlemen were well-founded," after all. The late spring of 1911 had been unusually cool and damp in the upper Sacramento Valley, and although Redding papers kept studiously quiet about it the region apparently had suffered a terrible burning from sulfur dioxide. The farmers' attorney also referred to "the blasting effect that has marked that country since the filing of the affidavits."

Balaklala's lawyer insisted that the company honestly felt it had lived up to the spirit of the 1910 agreement and had not done the farmers any economic damage, and still believed it was on the verge of conforming strictly with the terms of the smoke decree. "Of course, this entire proposition on so large a scale was an experiment, and in order to deal with the experiment, operation of the plant was necessary." He pointed out that one of the farmers' tests showed the efficiency of the Cottrell smoke consumer reaching as high as 96 percent. In response, Shanahan said it was not the maximum efficiency of the process that constituted protection, nor even did its average efficiency mean much to the injured parties; rather it was "the dreadful minimum of efficiency that constitutes the awful danger to a community situated as ours is with reference to this smelter." Judge Morrow directed Balaklala to pay the farmers $4,000 to cover the cost of the chemical investigation and costs of court, and he ordered the company to cease operations within thirty-five days, giving it leave only to work up the ore still in its bunkers as long as it did not exceed ten thousand tons.[36]

---

[36] "Appearances, Tuesday, June 20th, 1911," in NDC 15123.

The proindustry press had its predictable comments about the "uncompromising antagonism" of the Shasta farmers and how their "narrow policy" had just torpedoed a promising enterprise. "Large potential capital is locked in the ground in unproductive form, live capital has been sunk in a plant that cannot be used, a flourishing industry has been killed," bawled a report to San Francisco's Commonwealth Club. "This is the price that has been paid to protect a limited agricultural industry from an uncertain amount of damage." But in fact the Balaklala company had been treading water financially ever since its organization and undoubtedly was happy for an excuse to shut down at this time. It had been capitalized in the heady days just before the 1907 bust and ever since had been struggling to carry a big floating debt and pay off heavy construction and development costs, while moving its product in a sluggish market and clearing little better than a penny a pound. In 1908 it tried to bail itself out by floating $1.5 million in short-term bonds; in 1910 it had to levy a $1.25-a-share assessment on its stockholders. The company netted only $127,000 in the eighteen months ending June 1911, a pretty meager showing for a $4 million investment, certainly well short of the $40,000-a-month earnings first envisioned by its promoters. It had spent $108,000 on the Cottrell device and had been out $42,000 settling damage claims during the period. Although the smoke trouble undeniably bit into what otherwise might have been distributed as profit, a forensic accountant never would conclude it was the fatal agent in the smelter's demise.[37]

"The trouble between the farmers and the smelters" likewise offered a plausible straw to grasp when the Bank of

---

[37] *Redding Courier-Free Press*, April 7, May 4, 16, July 20, 1911; *Transactions of the Commonwealth Club of California* 7 (1912), 221; *Engineering and Mining Journal* 91 (1911), 481; *Mining World*, 35 (1911), 557; *Copper Handbook* 10 (1910–11), 390, 813; Austin, "Mining Investment Values," 109–12.

Shasta County, a million-dollar institution on paper, admitted a $224,000 deficiency and closed its doors that spring. "That trouble has cut off $125,000 monthly from the payrolls of the county during the last year and a half," spluttered the bank's president, although state examiners soon revealed that the real source of the difficulty was a string of ill-considered loans to various ill-savored mining and lumbering start-ups in the region. As the county grand jury was handing up indictments against the bank's officers, the Balaklala company was unconcernedly wrapping up its operations at Coram. The plant's expert machinists and electricians were reassigned to the Guggenheim operations in Chile, while hundreds of common stiffs dispersed in all directions with nowhere in particular to go. Just a handful of custodians and night watchmen stayed on the company payroll. By August 1911, Coram was virtually a ghost town, and the marshal of the place whiled away what was left of his term shooting the scores of hungry dogs and cats that had been left behind in the exodus and now were making pests of themselves. It had been home to over two thousand people in its heyday; now not even fifty souls hung on there, and choice business lots that recently sold for thousands were going begging. Insurance agents had promptly canceled their fire policies in the hapless town, knowing from long experience that arson was a favorite path of deliverance for merchants and property owners in mining settlements that suddenly played out.[38]

That was the summer that Ishi—"The Last Wild Indian in North America," in the circus-posterish tag of contemporary papers—stumbled into the sweet light of the twentieth century from his covert in the chaparral of the neighboring county. "Old Sam," an aged Yana who still lived on the river

[38] *Redding Courier-Free Press*, March 23, 27, April 5, June 17, 21, 24, 1911; *Redding Searchlight*, June 22, August 2, 8, 1911.

below Keswick, was hired to interpret for the poor devil. Nobody suggested that smelter smoke had been a factor in driv-
ing Ishi from his thicket, but elsewhere in the state it was a
source of growing irritation and agitation. The ranchers of
Amador, Calaveras, and San Joaquin counties had just organized a protective league of their own and were pressing
their dilatory supervisors to do something about the Penn
copper smelter at Campo Seco, in the Sierra Nevada foothills
east of Lodi. The farmers around Benicia were losing patience with Solano County's long-drawn-out injunction proceedings against the Selby smelter. Some filed suits of their
own against the Selby company only to learn that sometime
before it had quietly disincorporated and moved over to the
state of Nevada to reorganize, all with the aim of making itself less accessible to such actions. That spring Benicia's assemblyman had introduced a bill in Sacramento authorizing
state intervention in the smelter smoke problem. It managed
to clear the assembly after considerable parliamentary ma-
neuvering by its author, but the mining interests finally
clubbed it down when it reached the senate. In Shasta
County the farmers well understood that their vigilance
could not be relaxed any time soon. Business at the year-end
meeting of the farmers' protective association was perfunctory and quickly disposed of, but the mood was tentative and
uneasy, far from jolly. "While there was a general feeling of
satisfaction, it was decided that the executive committee
should keep a watchful eye and note results in the spring."[39]

---

[39] *Redding Courier-Free Press*, March 10, 13, 16, 21–22, December 8–9, 1911; *Redding Searchlight*, September 2, 1911; *Benicia Herald*, March 24, 31, 1911. See also Limbaugh and Fuller, *Calaveras Gold*, 245–46.

CHAPTER FOUR

"They continue, serenely, to destroy, devastate, and kill"

Shasta County farmers did not have long to bask in the glow of their superficial victory over Balaklala. The 1912 crop season was barely under way, but dissatisfaction with the re-sults of the agreement with Mammoth was already setting in. Anxieties and animosities that had never really quieted down started foaming again with fresh evidence that smelter fumes were still doing mischief. The ill effects of sulfur diox-ide were showing up in the new alfalfa and grain around An-derson, and the olive orchards around Olinda were dropping their leaves mysteriously. Apologists for Mammoth blamed the widespread withering of vegetation on the long, dry win-ter and recent cold north winds, but they had no explanation for the white crust, suggestive of acid corrosion, that had formed on fence wires all over the district. In March the ex-ecutive committee of the farmers' protective association went up to Kennett to lay their grievances before the com-pany. General Manager Metcalfe was on hand to explain the various adjustments and improvements that had been made at the baghouse. The farmers went away mollified if uncon-vinced. McCoy Fitzgerald denied that they intended any new legal action.[1]

---

[1] *Redding Courier-Free Press*, March 26–27, 1912.

Copper was back up to sixteen cents in the spring of 1912, and the smelters were itching to take advantage of the improving market situation. Mammoth quickly erected a new bank of cooling pipes and by summer had its third furnace back in permanent commission. In April Balaklala's vice president came to Redding to outline a possible new deal with the farmers' protective association, in hopes of getting a second chance for the smelter at Coram. The company offered to establish a permanent indemnity fund of $250,000, out of which damages would be awarded by an arbitration committee mutually appointed by the smelter and the farmers. The company also proposed to demolish its 250-foot brick smokestack at Coram and replace it with one less than half as high—the idea being to reduce the radius of smoke distribution, hopefully confining it to the already denuded canyon and sparing the agricultural lands below. On taking it up for consideration the farmers' executive committee gave "no indication of acceptance," and when the offer was presented to a general meeting of the members later in the month it was voted down decisively. The same meeting resolved in favor of initiating contempt proceedings against Mammoth, but the will of the majority was temporarily curbed by McCoy Fitzgerald, who cautioned that the association's treasury still was depleted from the previous year's action against Balaklala and very heavy expenditures would be necessary in a fresh tilt. Dues already stood at $1.25 per each $100 of the assessed valuation of each member's property.[2]

Vague in some instances, in some cases very pronounced, injury to crops and vegetation continued to augment, and with it the mutterings of the farmers. Several times over the course of the season the protective association notified Mammoth's management that damage was still being done. In De-

---

[2] Ibid., April 6, 1912; *Redding Searchlight*, April 6, 1912; *Engineering and Mining Journal* 93 (1912), 953; *Mining and Engineering World* 36 (1912), 1008.

Sacramento canyon below Coram in 1932, thirteen years after last copper smelter shut down. Scattered poison oak and manzanita. Photograph by A. E. Wieslander. Image 272,846 (Quadrangle 23), Vegetation Type Analysis Photographs, Bioscience and Natural Resources Library, University of California, Berkeley.

cember 1912, the exasperated members turned out McCoy Fitzgerald and the rest of the original executive committee and elected a whole new slate of officers, all of them known militants who could be trusted to make a decisive move against the smelter. It now seemed a foregone conclusion that the controversy would be thrown back in the courts again before long. It was known that Mammoth for two years past had kept a staff of experts busy organizing counterevidence in anticipation of this turn of events, and presumably the company was ready and able to take care of itself.[3]

---

[3] John E. Raker to attorney general, August 5, 1913, enclosing letter of Wm. J. Hill to Congressman Raker, October 9, 1912, in DOJ 144276; *Redding Courier-Free Press*, December 14, 1912.

As expected, the turn of the year saw the launching of an energetic campaign against the smelter. Appeals to the U.S. Department of Justice brought the cool reply that the federal government "has not authority to litigate for the benefit of individuals." How was it, one farmer reproachfully asked, that the same class of men the government claimed to have no authority to help were the first ones expected to "go to scrap for Uncle Sam anytime he is in trouble"? The protective association also endeavored to start some action by the state government, and there had somewhat better luck. In January 1913, a delegation had an audience with Assemblyman J. W. Stuckenbruck of San Joaquin County, who was conferring with farmers in his district who demanded California's assistance in their struggle with the Penn copper smelter at Campo Seco. Stuckenbruck drew up two bills on the farmers' behalf and introduced them in that session of the state legislature. The first bill, submitted in January 1913, apparently was regarded by the mining and smelting people as the less threatening of the two. It appropriated $5,000 for an expert commission to study alleged smelter damage in California, and if the final report was adverse obligated the governor to direct the attorney general to institute suits for abatement in the name of the people of the state. It cleared the assembly agriculture committee with little controversy and was passed by the legislature and signed by the governor in May. "The People" never would appear as plaintiff, but the California Smelter Wastes Commission would generate some excellent documentation of the environmental damage taking place.[4]

Stuckenbruck's other bill, introduced in March 1913, would have required all smelters and chemical works in California to be licensed and supervised by the state board of

---

[4] W. R. Harr to Chum Gibson, November 4, 1912, in DOJ 144276; *Redding Courier-Free Press*, January 22, May 12, 1913; California Legislature, *Final Calendar of Legislative Business*, 715.

health, which was to be given full authority to receive complaints and make inspections, to prescribe allowable discharges of sulfur, arsenic, "or any injurious substance"—and
if need be, to summarily shut down any plant found in violation of its orders. This proposal became the subject of hard
lobbying by both sides, although the hearings were largely
overshadowed by the Alien Land Bill and other controver-
sial "Anti-Jap" legislation then wending its way through the
state assembly. "It would put a potential weapon in the hands
of malicious or predatory persons, who for one reason or another desired to harass the smelting companies," said the
Oakland Tribune. "This would make business for blackmailers and shyster lawyers, but it would probably drive every
smelter out of the State." The smelting interests clearly were
afraid it would establish a process whose outcome could not
be so easily controlled. The bill's opponents held it up as long
as possible in the assembly mining committee, which happened to be chaired by Redding's assemblyman, C. W.
White. Although it finally reached the assembly floor and
passed with a solid majority, when it got up to the senate it
was effectively smothered after first reading in the public
health committee. "Conservation through legislation seems
uncalled for in this particular field," sniffed the Commonwealth Club of California. "Rather let us have legislation
that would promote development and free the industries
from vexatious litigation."[5]

The Shasta farmers' experience with their county government was entirely barren of results. In March 1913, a delegation from the protective association went before the county
board of supervisors to request a $2,000 appropriation to help

___

[5] *Redding Courier-Free Press*, March 19, April 5, 12, 17, 25, 1913; California Legislature,
Final Calendar of Legislative Business, 965. The mining lobby in Sacramento simultaneously thwarted an effort to regulate the gold-dredging industry in the Sierra Nevada
foothills: see Hichborn, *Story of the Session of the California Legislature of 1913*, 174–87.

with the contemplated litigation. They also urged that the district attorney be assigned to handle the proceedings as part of his official duties—this, after all, was what Solano County had done in Benicia's showdown with the Selby smelter. The farmers' mien was resolute, their speeches fervid, and their logic plain, but the nimble supervisors dodged the issue by referring it to the district attorney, who conveniently was out of town and unavailable for comment. In April the farmers presented their complaints to the county grand jury, which duly made an investigation and reported to the superior court at the end of the month. Its finding, expected to be perfunctory, was completely unfavorable to the smelter and hit "like a bolt from the blue." The grand jury determined that great detriment had been done to lands and crops over a large portion of the county, and that the evil was of such a character and occurred to such an extent as to merit being called a public nuisance. The jurors' examination of lands attached to the county hospital and poor farm showed that serious injury extended to the county's own property, and they concluded that county officials should be directed to take steps to abate the nuisance. "And we further find that the damage which is being done at the present time has been continuing for some time past and that the said board of supervisors has not so instructed the district attorney, nor has our district attorney called the matter to the attention of the board of supervisors, which in our mind should have been done." With notable presence and alacrity this time, the district attorney announced his opinion that public funds could not be appropriated for private purposes, and the farmers' claim that county action was being solicited to resolve a problem of general concern to the county's people did not alter the circumstance. That seemed to end the matter at this level.[6]

The Shasta County grand jury's finding fell short of an in-

---

[6] *Redding Courier-Free Press*, March 6, April 19, May 9, 1913.

dictment, but condemnation by a grand jury did tend to create a certain embarrassment for the Mammoth smelter, and
the smelter's friends, ever sensitive to good public relations,
did their level best to counteract it. The Mining Congress
of Northern California and Southern Oregon was set to con-
vene the following month in Redding and the city had
timed a "May Carnival" to coincide with it, turning the af-
fair into a general booster gala. As a crowning feature of the
festivities the promoters arranged a grand automobile tour of
the smoke zone. Leading the caravan was a new Cadillac
carrying an "investigating committee" composed of the state
mineralogist, one of the county supervisors, and three
prominent local mining men. At the end of the day the investigators presented their report, which stated that they
had "carefully and faithfully" studied local crop prospects
and found them "splendid"—in fact, "better than in other
sections of the State." They declared that they were "unan-
imous in the conclusion that, as at present conducted, the
smelting of ores can have no perceptible effect upon any
kind or character of vegetation," and they urged that "the
convention should give the fullest publicity to these self-evident facts." The convention obliged on the spot, passing a
resolution "that this Congress does hereby condemn the unnecessary agitation seeking to hamper the operations of
smelting in this district."[7]

Friends of the smelter went forth to spread the fullest publicity they could in magazines of national circulation. A
mendacious report in New York's prestigious *Engineering and
Mining Journal* proclaimed that Shasta County was rich in
agriculture despite any fumes, that there was no such damage
to crops as claimed, and that the present antismelter agitation was completely unjustified. "In most of the cases the
farmers have simply tried to put one over on the smelters,"

[7] Ibid., May 24, 26, 1913.

an accompanying editorial commented. "Public sentiment is, without sufficient reason, opposed to smelters, and jurors and court officers are only too ready to mulct them heavily whenever there is opportunity," Herbert Lang told sympathetic readers of San Francisco's *Mining and Scientific Press.* "They are looked upon almost as public enemies, and their operations are regarded as a public nuisance." Lang explained how the smelters' conscientious efforts to find a way to wash, strain, absorb, condense, or otherwise remove the sulfur from their smoke unfortunately had all proved unfeasible—feasibility meaning, first and foremost, commercial feasibility. Perfect fume control would have to await such time as the market could take up the acid or other by-products that the smelters would be generating, and until then the public would have to accept the industry's apologies and try to understand. "No one regrets this waste more than do the smelters, and they are fully alive to the desirability of conserving all valuable material and abolishing the nuisance. The public should realize what they do not seem to have grasped as yet, that the matter is a most difficult one, without the easy solution that the uninitiated appear to believe in." Of course in the meantime "it is not to be expected that owners of mines will suffer them to lie idle in order to conserve a substance of only problematic value when they are in position to realize on the more immediately valuable metals which they possess."

"It is very desirable now to do the utmost toward building up a public sentiment which will look with toleration upon their efforts," continued Lang, and he thought the public gladly would extend such toleration were it not for the pestilent agitation of "a certain class of our small landed proprietors" and their coadjutors, "pettyfogging lawyers of small calibre." Lang sketched the character of the "smoke farmer," the cunning rustic too shiftless to plow or prune, preferring instead to extort trumped-up indemnities from the unfortunate smelter in his neighborhood by terrorizing it with threats of injunction. "Noting the helpless condition of the smelters, a class of despicable blackmailers has grown up, who levy tribute on the industry, assisted by undiscriminating laws, and the profession of smoke-farming has attained quite a vogue," he gravely wrote. "A smoke-farmer is an agriculturalist who makes two spears of grass grow in place of one, so that if they providentially wither he may get paid for three," he went on. "By tying a sick horse in the path of smelter smoke he makes the price of two good horses when the poor beast expires. A barren ranch in the region of smoke is worth more than a fertile one in any other locality."[8]

That slur came to the attention of one of the sparkier complainants, Charles Paige, a lifelong Republican who promptly delivered a counterblast in vintage Populist style. "Smoke farmer is a choice and peculiar epithet," he sneered, "and it is almost a pity to find it merely a dishonest term in use by liars to stigmatize pioneer settlers and good citizens who are trying to protect their homes, property, and lives against the brutality of organized exploitation and vandalism." The suggestion that companies linked to the most powerful and ruthless industrial and financial syndicates in the world meekly submitted to shakedowns at the hands of a few poor hill farmers was rank absurdity:

> Do you, Mr. Editor, believe that there is such a person as a "smoke farmer" who blackmails smelting corporations? Do you believe that any corporation or industry in the West submits to extortion, as alleged by Mr. Lang? If you do, and hold opinion with those abused and mulcted corporate endeavors, with your combined resources and ability, why have you not, or why can you not, make an awful example of one of them? You certainly cannot plead that the law is deaf to corporation prayers in this State, or this

---

[8] Eddy, "What Has Been the Fume Damage in California?" 153–55; Lang, "Common Sense of the Fume Question," 341–44.

country. You certainly have as much shelter and protection by
courts and juries as is enjoyed by the miserable desert rancher who
assails, according to Mr. Lang, these interests by "tying a sick horse
in the path of the smelter smoke, and makes the smelter pay the
price of two good ones for killing one."

Mr. Editor, do you not know that all efforts to suppress what is
widely known to be a destructive nuisance of the worst character
have been repeatedly defeated in California? Do you not know that
the federal government is defied by the smelter interests? That state
government is helpless or inert? That county grand juries and local
organizations are a laughing stock and joke with these corporations?

"The defense of the smelting people is wonderfully simple," Paige concluded, "so much so that it looks like a slur
upon American intelligence and common sense. Admitting
that their smoke can be made harmless by various processes,
they say the by-products obtained will not pay the expense.
In other words, their reply to the unfortunate public is that
they prefer still to employ agents, attorneys, and flunkies to
cover up, befog, and prostitute, while they continue, serenely,
to destroy, devastate, and kill." A Denver mining journal observed that the farmer-smelter conflict in California was
starting to take on the features of a regular class war, and
rhetorically at least this certainly appeared to be the case.[9]
By the summer of 1913 it was evident that the bountiful
harvests forecast by the gentlemen of the mining congress
that spring were not going to materialize. Pears were an outright disaster, the growers scowling at a crop that appeared to
be just a fraction of the previous year's bad crop. It was remarked that the county's pear orchards were "fast fading
away," and some feared that Anderson would be shipping
none of the fruit at all in a few years. The prune crop also
was quite dismal, and the fact that dried fruit prices were
strong only made the situation more frustrating. In July a big
wildfire, two miles wide in places, swept the desiccated brush

---

[9] *Mining and Scientific Press* 107 (1913), 540; *Mining Reporter* 68 (1913), 9–11.

and scrub of Happy Valley, burning fences and destroying a number of small orchards. Later that month the district experienced another alarming defoliation of native vegetation. In a wide belt of foothill country east and west of Redding the leaves on all varieties of oak trees suddenly shriveled and dropped off. Mammoth's friends were quick to proclaim that "smelter smoke has had nothing to do with the blight." In the absence of any evident infection or insect problem, they blamed the situation on the "scorching effect" of the "high north winds of two weeks ago."[10]

An additional worry to the farmers that summer was another bid by the Balaklala company to reopen its smelter. The company's general manager came west in July 1913 with a consulting engineer and a dozen expert mechanics. It was disclosed that the company contemplated resuming operations at Coram using a promising but unproven fume-control process recently patented by a Brooklyn chemist. The company manager immediately started in with blandishments: "Not only will we do no damage, but we want you in addition to satisfy yourselves that no damage will be done." In a month Balaklala had sixty men working on preliminary repairs and modifications at the smelter, and drilling teams were busy knocking down big quantities of ore up at the company mine.[11]

A general meeting of the farmers' protective association at the end of August 1913 voted to raise a $10,000 war chest. The organization was without legal counsel at the time, and it also was anticipated that chemical experts would have to be retained on a permanent basis. A resumption of smelting at Coram not only would mean a great deal more smoke, but also would make the problem of assigning responsibility for damages a great deal trickier. The farmers repeatedly had written to their congressman and to various departments in

---

[10] *Redding Courier-Free Press*, July 12, 21, August 6, 1913.

[11] Ibid., July 8, August 14, 18, 1913; Wierum, "Experimental Development of the Hall Process," 518–21.

Washington, trying to stir some federal agency to take a hand somehow in their predicament. In an attempt to quiet their complaints, John A. Holmes, director of the U.S. Bureau of Mines, swung through Redding on his way home from Alaska in October and talked with a group of restless association members. They told him how crops and timber still were suffering from Mammoth's smoke, how the evil effects occasionally were traceable as far south as eighty miles, well into the neighboring county. Holmes was able to give them nothing but reassurances, telling them that his bureau had thirty men studying possible technical solutions and that he hoped a "happy termination" of the difficulty was not too many years off. Shortly after that the executive committee of the protective association concluded to hire attorneys to bring an action against the smelter. They contacted Francis J. Heney, lion of the prosecution in the sensational San Francisco graft trials a few years before, but were unable to meet the price he wanted for his services. Mammoth meanwhile was forging ahead with development work, seemingly unperturbed. In November it bought a group of twenty-one new claims, and it took an option on another group of thirty-five claims a few weeks later.[12]

The state's smelter wastes commission put its first investigator in the field that fall. George P. Weldon, chief deputy of the California Commission of Horticulture, made a four-day reconnaissance of the Shasta smoke belt in November 1913. His preliminary size-up was decidedly unfavorable to the Mammoth company. At Kennett he watched clouds of smoke rising continuously from the smelter, clearly showing that the fume-control system was nowhere close to being as

[12] *Redding Searchlight*, August 31, October 19, 1913; *Redding Courier-Free Press*, October 17, November 18–19, December 5, 1913. See also Bean, *Boss Ruef's San Francisco*, 305–306. The "misjoinder" pitfall—the legal and technical problem of identifying just who was responsible for just what—had been fatal to the plaintiffs in similar cases in the not-so-distant past: see, for example, Kelley, *Gold vs. Grain*, 106–23.

efficient as the company bragged. Miles of barren hills surrounding the plant testified to ongoing as well as past injury.
Although the baghouse had been in commission for over
three years, grass and herbage were making no show at all to
reestablish themselves, and a perfectly green and healthy tree
or shrub was not to be found. Weldon figured that severe
smoke damage affected a belt of territory at least twelve miles
wide, stretching from a point five or six miles above Kennett
clear down to Anderson, a total distance of thirty-five miles.
Mammoth furnished a car and driver to take him far out into
a neighboring county to look at a mildew on the native oaks,
which the company said was indistinguishable from the
markings many blamed on smelter fumes. "It does not take
an expert to note the difference, however, and their point is
certainly a weak one." They also ushered him to a number of
select spots not far from the smelter, where gardens flour-
ished, patches of native timber survived, or other conditions
obtained "which the smelter officials are glad to tell the
stranger about." Mr. Weldon remained unimpressed. He concluded that such anomalies merely represented sheltered
topographic pockets or other chance, favorable circumstances. "It must be admitted that while a few unexplainable
cases such as this can be found, the evidence against present
injury is not of any great consequence, in comparison with
the evidence for it." Further investigation was put off till the
following spring, when the problem of detecting smoke injury would not be complicated by fall tints or the effects of
summer drought.[13]

The weather was rather severe in December 1913. When
the farmers around Redding cried that their young wheat had
been burned almost to the ground by smelter fumes, Mammoth's friends could point to successive heavy frosts and an

---

[13] Geo. P. Weldon, "Report of Smelter Fumes Investigation, Redding, Cal., Nov. 5th–
8th, 1913," in "Affidavit Showing Necessity for Inspection of Smelter," October 16, 1914,
in NDC 15122.

inch of ice standing on local reservoirs. At the end of the
month one of the heaviest storms in years swept in. The
creeks boomed, the river went up seventeen feet at Redding,
and in the denuded area between Redding and Kennett there
were at least seven major landslides. At one point below
Coram a quarter-mile section of the Southern Pacific track
was buried eight feet deep by a flood of mud and rocks. It
made a dramatic and rather appropriate backdrop for a protective association meeting that finalized the engagement of
Charles Braynard and Theodore Bell as attorneys for the
farmers. Braynard had been a cynosure of local progressives
since 1911, when as Redding's city attorney he boldly re-
opened the case of a teenage tramp who had been beaten to
death by a company "bull" in the Redding train yards. A rail-
road-controlled coroner and district attorney had dismissed
the murder as accidental, but Braynard forced it before the
county grand jury then licked a vindictive charge of jury-
tampering leveled against him by the local establishment.
Bell, who hailed from Napa, enjoyed a much wider celebrity.
He had been the Democratic candidate for governor in both
1906 and 1910 and still played a prominent role in state and
national party politics. Perhaps politics was his reason for
getting mixed up in this controversy, but Bell was recognized
as a committed scrapper with a certain fatal hankering for
underdog causes—his defending the Berkeley disloyalty cases
in 1918 virtually ended his political career.[14]

By April 1914 the mood of the majority in the farmers'
protective association definitely was in favor of action. After
the light yields of 1913 Anderson area prune growers had
been looking forward to a rebound; instead they found themselves confronted with a total crop failure. There was no
question of drought or frost, and heavy blossoming earlier in

---

[14] *Redding Courier-Free Press*, December 18, 31, 1913, *Redding Searchlight*, January 23,
1914; *San Francisco Chronicle*, October 31, 1918; Stadtman, *The University of California,
1868–1968*, 195.

the spring had presaged a banner year, and yet the fruit set had failed absolutely. Some imaginative theorists suggested a "change in the atmosphere" due to Lassen Peak's recent belchings, but somehow this idea did not gain much traction. Growers remembered that breezes from the north had prevailed while the trees were in bloom and accordingly traced the debacle to smelter fumes. Angry ranchers cornered the county board of supervisors for several hours one afternoon in May, badgering them once again—once again unsuccessfully—for an appropriation to help defray the expenses of the pending thrust against Mammoth. At a cost of nearly $3,000, the protective association already had engaged Western Laboratories of Oakland to take samples and run tests. The tests were carried out in June, July, and August, and the results were presented in September.[15]

At the smelter, the Western Laboratories men set up scaffolds and installed sampling pipes in the big towers above the baghouse, where they made numerous tests of the exit gases. Stack emissions of sulfur dioxide were found to be within the 0.75 percent limit set forth in the 1910 court decree, although a great deal of smoke carrying much more than that was found to be escaping from the ventilator openings under the eaves of the baghouse. Small amounts of sulfur trioxide and sulfuric acid were detected in each sample, which was in technical violation of the decree's restrictions and quite contrary to the smelter management's claim that those compounds were being completely eliminated. But the really salient problem, the report correctly pointed out, was that the smelter was incinerating over three hundred tons of raw sulfur a day, which converted to over six hundred tons of sulfur dioxide a day, and no effort at all was made to retain this enormous volume of noxious gas, the company satisfying

---

[15] *Redding Courier-Free Press*, April 23, May 7–8, 1914; *Redding Searchlight*, May 8, 1914; *Engineering and Mining Journal* 97 (1914), 1311.

its conscience by diluting it with fans to keep the concentration at point of exit below the maximum specified in the decree, seventy-five hundred parts per million. Yet it was well established that sulfur dioxide concentrations of as little as one part per million could injure plants significantly, and the fact that people living in the region often were conscious of its presence by smell, suggesting a field concentration of at least three parts per million, showed that it often descended in amounts concentrated enough to do damage. The chemists from Western Laboratories took clippings from native and cultivated plants on farms as far away as twenty-three miles from the Kennett smelter. The material was tested for sulfur and arsenic content, and the results were consistent enough—uniformly greater in certain directions and within a certain zone—to indicate extensive contamination by smelter fumes. The poisons constantly settling out of the air not only were destructive to growing vegetation, the report observed, but also probably had a detrimental effect on soil chemistry and soil organisms and hence on the long-term fertility of the farmers' lands.

The Western Laboratories investigators also determined that the elimination of particulate matter by the baghouse was much less efficient than the Mammoth management boasted. "Clouds of smoke can be observed each and every day rising from the stacks or towers above the bag house. Smoke can also be seen rising almost continuously from the building where the furnaces are located." Great quantities of visible dust escaped during and after each vigorous shaking of the bags, an operation performed at least four times a day. Moreover, an appreciable amount of dust was continually slipping through the system, forced through by the powerful draft of the fans. At any given time many bags in the complex were weakened or torn and so were holding back little or no dust. The fumes going up the stacks and out over the

countryside this way contained between 6 and 7 percent arsenic. Analysis of the raw ore indicated that as much as two
tons of arsenic were volatilized every day in the smelting operation. The Western Laboratories report decided that the
baghouse really was doing nothing to prevent smoke damage, except to the extent that it reduced the concentration
of fumes in the immediate vicinity of the smelter. It concluded that the Mammoth company was in violation of the
1910 court decree "beyond the possibility of a doubt," and if
the company was unable to find means to correct the situation "then it should be compelled to cease operations."[16]

Those unequivocal conclusions were just what the farmers were waiting for. In October 1914 they petitioned the district court in San Francisco for a contempt ruling against
Mammoth, charging the company with violating five of the
six provisions of the 1910 decree. Their affidavit referred to
the damning report by Western Laboratories, as well as to
the adverse finding of the Shasta County grand jury the year
before, and also to Bulletins 89 and 113 of the U.S. Department of Agriculture's Bureau of Chemistry, published in 1905
and 1910, which concluded that even very minute amounts
of sulfur dioxide could damage vegetation severely. The company made answer the following month, insisting that there
had been no economic damage from smelter emanations
since the Balaklala plant shut down in July 1911, and that all
injuries now complained of either were incurred before that
time or were the result of natural causes. The company said
it consistently had maintained its sulfur dioxide discharges at
strengths below the 0.75 percent maximum stipulated in the
1910 smoke decree, and pointed out that the publications
cited to show that the stipulated limit was not good enough
had been available to the plaintiffs at the time they con-

---

[16] Exhibits B and D, in "Petition for Rule to Show Cause for Contempt," October 16,
1914, in NDC 15122.

sented to the decree. It submitted a chart showing how the total quantity of sulfide ores smelted in Shasta County had declined from a peak of almost a million tons in 1910 to little more than three hundred thousand tons in the present season. Let us note that a fairly serious industrial recession was on at the time—in fact the Mammoth smelter had been shut down much of that fall.[17]

Mammoth's engineers and chemists insisted that natural neutralization of the smoke thanks to the ore's zinc oxide content was perfect, so precluded the presence of sulfur trioxide or sulfuric acid, and therefore the determination by Western Laboratories of those compounds in the stack gases could not have been correct. They asserted that the filtration of solids from the smoke stream was virtually 99 percent efficient, the twenty-five thousand-ton dust pile standing in the smelter yard bearing witness to the fact. The shaking of the bags, they said, always was done carefully, just one section at a time with the flow of smoke diverted to other sections, and except when strong crosswinds were blowing what escaped was "only in minute quantities, appearing as the thinnest haze." As to sulfur dioxide releases, their records showed they had been keeping the average strength at 0.59 percent, well below the maximum stipulated in the 1910 decree, and at this concentration surrounding vegetation never would be damaged. The sulfur dioxide was dissipated rapidly by mixing and diffusion in the general atmosphere, they claimed, and did not condense and settle to earth in the form of sulfuric acid as the plaintiffs believed. That spring and summer the company had tested the atmosphere at various stations around the area. At the Hotel Redding sulfur dioxide exceeded one part per million only four of twenty-seven days; on January Creek, a mile north of town, it reached that

[17] "Affidavit Showing Necessity for Inspection of Smelter," October 16, 1914, and "Answer to Affidavit Showing Necessity for Inspection," November 30, 1914, in NDC 15122.

level only fifteen of eighty-six days. Exactly what comfort these figures were supposed to represent is unclear.[18]

Along with its answer the company filed fifty supporting affidavits, thirty-seven of which were from rural property owners in the Redding, Anderson, and Happy Valley vicinities. They ranged from the immigrant market gardener who claimed to have grossed $2,000 off his fourteen acres and so considered that he had nothing to complain about, to the San Francisco capitalist who had just conveyed seventeen hundred acres for subdivision and swore that no discount had been asked or offered because of smelter smoke. All of them vouched for a great improvement in conditions under the baghouse regime and claimed that alfalfa and barley, peaches and prunes, and oaks and grasses were all growing robustly again. Some claimed to be so encouraged that they were planning to clear new ground for farming. A number of them were erstwhile members of the farmers' protective association who protested that they had been named as parties to this action without their knowledge or consent, and stated that they presently believed the Mammoth company had kept faith and effectively controlled its smoke. All of them felt that closing the plant would be a serious loss "to their own interests, as well as to the general welfare."[19]

The company's little stable of credentialed agricultural experts also was ready with exculpatory statements. Professor Lewis Merrill, lately of the Utah Agricultural College but now a fulltime employee of the Mammoth Copper Company, swore that he saw no evidence whatsoever that damage was being done or that crops were being reduced by smelter emanations. On the contrary, it seemed to him that all signs of former injury were "constantly disappearing." Since 1911,

---

[18] Exhibits 13, 14, 16, and 17, in "Return and Answer of Defendant to Petition of Erle M. Downing, and Affidavits," November 30, 1914, in NDC 15122.

[19] Exhibits 24 and 39, in "Return and Answer of Defendant," in NDC 15122.

crops in the region had been perfectly normal and in many cases had been very good, and where they had not the problem often could be charged to poor soil. He also indicated some prevalent insect pests, like red spider and thrips, and certain plant diseases, notably fire blight and sclerotinia, that were responsible for significant losses. But by and large, Merrill emphasized, good yields almost always were commensurate with cultivation, irrigation, and other exertions on the part of the farmer, and poor yields with lack of same. Another Utah academic imported by the company that spring made substantially the same assertions. He had examined the wild vegetation of the Kennett vicinity and found it putting out lots of "healthy new growth." He concluded that "reforesting is rapidly taking place and new ground cover is appearing in the barren sections." The finding of alleged smelter poisons in the soil and vegetation of the smoke zone meant nothing at all, he declared, because sulfur and arsenic also could be found "in many virgin soils far removed from any unnatural source."[20]

The agronomic experts of the California Smelter Wastes Commission had hit the field in earnest in the spring of 1914. The farmers got access to their detailed reports and filed a copy as Plaintiff's Exhibit A—fifty pages typed single-space on legalcap sheets. The state investigators had focused special attention on the George Baker ranch, on the Sacramento River about a mile above Redding. This large property had suffered the most appalling deterioration, sitting right in the smoke's line of drift as it came funneling out of the canyon. A good-sized almond orchard on the place was practically worthless and no longer cared for, the trees full of dead wood from past injury and the fresh leaves of the present sea-

---

[20] Exhibits 38 and 40, in "Return and Answer of Defendant," in NDC 15122. Compare National Research Council, *Sulfur Oxides*, 82–86, 101–08; Walter W. Heck and C. Stafford Brandt, "Effects on Vegetation: Native, Crops, Forest," in Stern, *Air Pollution*, vol. 2, 164–67.

son already burned and dropping off. On the bottom land along the river, hundreds of elegant valley oaks were completely dead. Back on the surrounding hills practically all native vegetation was gone except for a little poison oak and manzanita. The rains were cutting the dirt and gravel from the barren slopes and washing it down onto the cultivated land. Baker had thickly seeded his fields to wheat the previous fall, but by March 1914 the stand was too scant to make a crop worth harvesting. Surviving plants, scattered over the ground, were bleached and stunted, and in many places a sickly white residue coated the soil. Galvanized fence wire that had been strung just five years before was almost completely eaten up and could be snapped easily with the fingers. For reasons plain to see, Baker was one of the most adamant antismelter activists. On his own account he recently had filed two damage suits against the Mammoth company, citing injuries totaling $35,000.

The state investigators proceeded farther downwind. Grass and clover lawns in the city of Redding, fifteen miles from the smelter, bore a queer silvery sheen from bleached leaf tips, and the foliage of rose bushes and other ornamental plants was blotched and spotted with the characteristic markings of sulfur dioxide. Shade trees and shrubbery around the town looked generally weak and dwarfish. On ranches outside the city and south to a distance of three or four miles, the grain and alfalfa fields as well as roadside weeds were all partially burned and discolored. It was not unusual to find 50 percent bleaching on the leaves of alfalfa plants, and in many instances the blades of oats and barley had been burned back as much as five inches from the tips. Old orchard trees still bore some fruit but looked yellow and unhealthy, and this condition seemed just as prevalent where trees had been regularly sprayed, pruned, and watered as where they had not. A few insect pests were noted, along with traces of various fun-

gal and bacterial diseases, but none seemed prevalent enough
to account for significant injury or retardation. Farther out,
on ranches five to ten miles south of the city, the appearance
of the fields was appreciably better but "not over-healthy."
Bleaching of leaves and other pronounced indications of sulfur dioxide injury were absent but crops clearly lacked proper
vigor and color. Around Anderson, fifteen miles south of
Redding and thirty miles from the smelter, crop conditions
seemed a little better yet—in fact "nearly normal," but still
somehow "not of the best." While the peach and pear crops
looked fairly decent this year, the prune set had failed completely, and all varieties of orchard trees seemed to be at a
standstill, with twigs and branches showing a tendency to
dieback that was only partially explained by blight or borers.

It was the abnormal appearance of the region's native
evergreen flora that most plainly told the state's investigators that "there exists some condition that is not favorable to
growing vegetation." It was something that hardly could be
blamed on poor husbandry or an unsuitable soil or climate.
From Redding down to Anderson and west to Happy Valley,
those gray pines that were not already dead were decidedly
unhealthy. They were pitifully thin in foliage, having but one
or two years' growth of needles instead of the normal three
to five years' growth. Many of the young needles on most of
the surviving trees were drying up at the tips and turning
brown. Sick pines were checked over carefully for pests, but
examination disclosed the presence of only one species that
might have had any pathological effect, an indigenous scale
insect, and this was by no means prevalent enough to account for the near-universal decline. The live oaks presented
a scraggly appearance and many of the limbs on them were
dead. Spring leaves that should have been a bright healthy
green were edged and speckled with necrotic spots. Here
again the few insects and fungal infections that were detected

on the oaks did not begin to explain their general unthrifti-
ness. Many native brush species were suffering likewise, although the manzanitas seemed to be withstanding the fumes'
influence fairly well.[21]

California's state forester, G. M. Homans, had spent several days studying range and woodland conditions south of
Redding. "Every rancher in this territory was firm in his con-
viction that smelter fumes had recently and were still burning trees on their respective properties," he reported, and his
personal examination of the evidence persuaded him that
this was indeed the case. "They state further that a portion
of their revenue is derived from the sale of wood and that
they are compelled to cut small dying trees, which, if unin-
jured, could be held until they attained a greater size. Dead
and dying trees must be marketed immediately otherwise the
wood is rejected." Homans, remembered by one historian as
"a rather cold personality," was warmly sympathetic. "Everyone is cutting their dead trees, necessitating the tying-up of
money needed for other purposes, while the excessive cut
swamps the market and reduces the price of cordwood."

The ranchers complained not just about the killing of native trees, but even more about depletion of the native range
far below normal carrying capacity. In some cases this appears
to have been severe indeed. At the 2,250-acre Saeltzer property southeast of Redding, Homans observed: "The ground
cover is very light and there is practically no reproduction of
any species. Everything appears sickly, and the range is no
longer capable of supporting stock." A year later this bot-
tomland estate would be sold off to an Oroville gold-dredging
outfit. A couple of miles up the road was the 445-acre

---

[21] For example Leroy Childs, "Report of General Crop Conditions, Insect Pests and
Fungous Diseases in the Vicinity of Redding, California, to Smelter Wastes Commission,"
in "Affidavit Showing Necessity for Inspection of Smelter," October 16, 1914, in NDC
15122. See also *Redding Searchlight*, October 31, 1914.

Kleineberg ranch, which had been depleted to such an extent that the owner had given up stock raising altogether. Purchased twenty-three years before for $15 an acre and assessed for years thereafter at $10 an acre, the place now was assessed at $1.50 an acre. Court records contain a pathetic appeal Kleineberg sent the smelters' management in 1910: "I find my timber ruined and gone, my grasses absolutely destroyed, so badly, that there is nothing at all left." Homans found conditions on the 685-acre Van Balveren ranch, on the river midway between Redding and Anderson, only slightly better: "His range appears unhealthy and the scanty ground cover is in an abnormal condition, the cause of which cannot be accounted for by the presence of stock, insects, or fungi. Much of his timber has been killed and many young trees have been so weakened that a speedy death seems inevitable."[22]

The situation in the smoke belt was compared to the situation around Red Bluff, fifteen miles south of Anderson and forty-five miles from the smelter, where soil and climate conditions as well as the incidence of plant pests and diseases were about the same. It readily was seen that general crop conditions were much more favorable outside the reach of smelter fumes. Red Bluff orchards were relatively free of withered shoots and dead twigs; growing grain was taller and greener, with far fewer dead leaves; alfalfa fields exhibited no bleached leaves; native gray pines were without all the dead needles. W. E. Burke of Stanford University was engaged by the Smelter Wastes Commission to see if chemical analysis could confirm what would be decided from general appearances. Burke found that barley and alfalfa samples collected around Anderson contained twice the sulfur of samples taken

[22] G. M. Homans, "Observations near Redding for Smelter Wastes Commission," in "Affidavit Showing Necessity," in NDC 15122; Clar, *California Government and Forestry*, 296; *Redding Courier-Free Press*, July 12, 1915; C. Kleineberg to "Mammoth and Balaklala Smelters," September 15, 1910, in NDC 15122.

around Red Bluff; samples from around Redding had three times more sulfur. Gray pine needles from the Redding vicinity had more than four times the sulfur of needles gathered around Red Bluff. The sulfur content of subsoil samples from the different locales tested constant within 0.01 percent. Burke concluded that the excessive quantities detected in foliage from the smoke belt had originated as sulfur dioxide absorbed from the polluted atmosphere and accurately reflected the extent of smelter fumes injury.[23]

Mammoth's refutations and counterclaims might have looked a bit rubbery alongside the stack of hard evidence offered by the farmers, but the company knew the burden of proof was on the petitioners, and this burden would be awkward indeed in a court that already had demonstrated its keen appreciation of the balance-of-injury doctrine and certainly did not care to be persuaded to rule against one of the state's great moneymaking enterprises. An article in the *Redding Searchlight* pointed out that the Mammoth company had produced over $33 million in copper, silver, and gold since it began operations in Shasta County, was presently employing a thousand men and distributing a payroll of $80,000 a month, and had built up a business whose closure would instantly strike more than a million dollars off the county's tax rolls.

The hearings were opened in December 1914 before Judge William Van Fleet in San Francisco, adjourned a few days so the judge personally could tour Kennett and the smoke belt, then resumed and lasted almost two weeks. The officers of the protective association came to the city with a crowd of other aggrieved farmers to relate their stories of the blighting effect of Mammoth's smoke on their crops and lands. The investigators from the Smelter Wastes Commission appeared

---

[23] W. E. Burke, "A Report to the Smelter Wastes Commission on the Chemical Investigation of Injury Done to Vegetation by Smelter Wastes in the Vicinity of Redding, California," in "Affidavit Showing Necessity," in NDC 15122.

before the court to testify and be crossexamined about the conditions they had found. Mammoth presented its own full slate of witnesses. Its experts criticized the findings of Western Laboratories as technically flawed and the reports of the California Smelter Wastes Commission as nothing more than collections of personal impressions. The issue was continued to February 1915 in order to close some other cases on the court's calendar, then postponed again so the two sides could put in small amounts of additional evidence.[24]

As it ended up, Judge Van Fleet's ruling, handed down on March 9, 1915, went completely against the farmers. Their application to have the smelter closed and the company charged with contempt was denied, and the costs of the whole proceeding were thrown back on the petitioners. The Mammoth company and its sympathizers went away rejoicing. The *Searchlight* eagerly looked for "the return of the golden days" and said the outcome of the case should be "hailed with delight by the majority, even though it be very displeasing to a few." Local ranchers must simply accept the higher judgment, face up to the new reality, and make the most of it, the paper chivalrously counseled. It only was to be hoped that their injuries, if any, eventually would be recouped and that they would reap their fair share of the prosperity that was going to come to the whole county with the full resumption of copper smelting. "The smelters may now operate under reasonable restrictions and big business and little business should proceed to make the most of it. Let the losses to one side be more than recompensated by the gains to the other."[25]

In fact the Mammoth company, and indeed the whole American copper industry, was on the verge of a boom the like of which it had not enjoyed in years. Operations had

---

[24] *Redding Searchlight*, October 17, 22, December 2–4, 8, 10, 12–13, 17–18, 20, 1914; February 26, 1915.

[25] Ibid., March 10–11, 1915.

been sharply curtailed the previous summer when the out-
break of hostilities in Europe and the British navy's black-
listing of copper as a contraband of war temporarily
disorganized world markets and sent the price plunging down
to 11 cents. Mammoth cut back from three furnaces to two
in August 1914, then shut down altogether for most of September. But by year's end Allied war orders were breathing a
whole new life into the situation. "Since there is no immediate prospect of peace among the nations of Europe, it is fair
to assume that the demand for copper will increase as the
conflict continues, and while it is a grewsome prospect to
contemplate, Shasta County's principal mineral industry will
be the gainer." In January 1915 Mammoth got its third furnace back in commission and soon was running full capacity,
putting through twelve hundred tons a day by March. The
company had taken advantage of the slowdown at the
smelter to hook up an even larger bank of cooling pipes and
finish other baghouse alterations and repairs which practically doubled the capacity of the plant. There was talk of
blowing in a fourth furnace, and the company hired three
hundred more miners to speed up development work on its
new properties. High war demand for zinc enabled the
smelter to ship out its enormous pile of baghouse waste to an
Oklahoma refining plant that summer for a reported
$160,000. The net profits of its parent company, United
States Smelting, Refining, and Mining, shot from $2.3 mil-
lion in 1914 to $6.5 million in 1915.[26]

Shasta County farmers woke up to the uncomfortable re-
alization that they had been outmaneuvered, and that the
signed agreement and federal court decree that were supposed to deliver them from smelter smoke had instead legit-

[26] *Engineering and Mining Journal* 99 (1915), 823; 101 (1916), 1063; *Redding Courier-Free Press*, August 10, September 26, 1914; July 22, August 14, 1915; *Mining and Engineering World* 42 (1915), 100; 43 (1915), 28, 338, 868; 44 (1916), 293.

imized and made perpetual the curse. The protective association stubbornly announced that it would continue the fight from a new angle and push for a final, favorable adjudication. The summary report of the California Smelter Wastes Commission had been laid on Governor Hiram Johnson's desk at the close of December 1914 over the signatures of Dr. Charles Keane, state veterinarian, Dr. Donald H. Currie, secretary of the state board of health, and Dr. A. J. Cook, state commissioner of horticulture. These officials called the ravages of smelter smoke in the Redding region "startling" and declared themselves "thoroughly convinced that very obvious and substantial loss to property owners is sustained." The farmers insisted that since the state commissioners' report established the fact that gross damage was being inflicted, the state of California was obligated under the legislative act which established the commission to bring an action for permanent abatement of the nuisance. Inquiries to the state attorney general brought assurances that "we expect to be in a position to take some proceedings very soon."[27]

But here again the farmers were going to be disappointed. Mammoth's resident manager asked the state attorney general for a stay of proceedings and an opportunity to present the results of the company's own "minute investigations of this entire situation." It seems the Smelter Wastes Commission had not followed through on a promise to grant the company a special hearing before filing its final report. Although the commissioners protested that such a hearing would have had "absolutely no bearing" on their findings, Attorney General U. S. Webb decided that official pledges should be honored in any case. At hearings in Sacramento in July 1915, the company presented a mess of testimony on its behalf and compelled the commission to reopen its investi-

---

[27] *Sacramento Union*, December 25, 1914; attorney general to L. E. Gibson, April 5, 1915, in California Attorney General Letter Books, 1906–1941, vol. 30, California State Archives, Office of Secretary of State, Sacramento, Calif.

gations. The commissioners mailed out questionnaires and made some additional inquiries the following month; after that the whole matter seems to have been quietly forgotten. By fall the California Smelter Wastes Commission's appropriation had been used up and it had for all practical purposes ceased to exist.[28]

"By and by the farmers will get tired of paying fees to attorneys and wake up to the fact that the courts cannot be fooled," the *Engineering and Mining Journal* smugly proclaimed. "The number of complaining farmers in Shasta County is gradually diminishing, it is encouraging to note." Yet the lingering embers of farmer hostility were still hot enough to persuade the Balaklala company to abandon plans to revive its smelter at Coram. In August 1915 it closed a ten-year contract to ship 250 tons of ore a day to the booming furnaces at Kennett for treatment on a custom basis. Mammoth's manager took the opportunity to point out that it was unlikely any other smelter would start up in the district as long as his plant was permitted to operate full swing. The farmers, increasingly dispirited and divided, at least could salvage that bit of comfort from the situation. Smelter fumes thickly shrouded Anderson at Easter, 1916, burning back the season's first cutting of alfalfa. "And still the smelter people laugh at the farmers and tell them they don't know what they are talking about," said the *Anderson Valley News*. The farmers, it bitterly reflected, surely would have carried their case had not many among them, enticed by the copper company's money, bolted from the ranks and sworn to false affidavits.[29]

Other developments came along to distract the farmers' attention and diffuse their rancor. Not long after Van Fleet's de-

---

[28] *Redding Searchlight*, July 25, 1915; *Redding Courier-Free Press*, July 27, August 9, 1915; attorney general to Hiram W. Johnson, July 2, 1915, in California Attorney General Letter Books, 1906–1941, vol. 31, and California Board of Health Secretary's Log, 1914–1922, 188, California State Archives, Office of Secretary of State, Sacramento, Calif.

[29] *Engineering and Mining Journal* 99 (1915), 551; *Redding Courier-Free Press*, August 20–21, 30, 1915; *Anderson Valley News*, April 6, 1916.

cision was handed down, the *Courier-Free Press* was vigorously pushing an enterprise called the "Field's Process Smelter Fumes Company." Alfred Field was a freelance Stockton inventor who had come to Redding with a new idea for the conversion and control of smelter smoke. He proposed to cool the furnace gases in bulk by means of long horizontal flues and a system of compressors and refrigerating towers. According to theory, the particulate elements in the fumes would be "frozen out" and precipitated into hoppers while the sulfur dioxide was recovered in fairly pure liquid form. Put up in tanks and carboys, the liquid sulfur dioxide would find a ready market nationwide as a cheap substitute for ammonia in industrial refrigeration. Field secured permission to set up a small experimental plant at the city gravel pit and raked together $6,000 for the initial work, most of it subscribed in small amounts by local farmers who were thrilled at something that promised to cure an evil and make money too.

The *Courier-Free Press* bullishly predicted that it was going to make Redding "one of the most important industrial communities of the Pacific Coast." Professional metallurgists and engineers tended to scoff at it as speculative and naive, however. The *Engineering and Mining Journal* said only that "it is a welcome experiment, even if it does nothing more than keep the farmers quiet." When Field and his partners tried to raise another $24,000 through a limited stock issue the state's blue-sky inspectors restricted them, requiring that the money accumulate in a closed account before any of it could be spent. Additional subscriptions were minimal, and the project stalled. In April 1916 the state commissioner of corporations advised holders of stock in the company of their right to recover their money. A year later the plant was sold to a local junk dealer for $150. Field was said to be somewhere in Oregon.[30]

---

[30] *Redding Courier-Free Press*, July 16, 1913; March 22, 24, 26, 1915; April 12, 1916; June 26, 1917; *Engineering and Mining Journal* 97 (1914), 923.

A much better founded project was the Anderson-Cottonwood Irrigation District, organized in 1914, favorably reported by the state engineer in 1915, and approved for a $480,000 bond issue the following January. Contracts were let and dirt started to fly that spring, and by summer several miles of the main canal had been completed. Local investors as well as outsiders immediately showed a lively interest in farm property in the 32,500-acre district, and prune orchards were trading hands at $200 an acre and more. County growers were reported to be "more than enthusiastic": the 1916 prune set looked surprisingly good and early bids were running over ten cents a pound, war demand having given the dried fruit market, like the copper market, a buoyancy that had been lacking for a long time. There is no reason to suppose overall smoke damage was any less, but a fortunate season certainly would have tended to allay any bad feelings. In any case, Mammoth's economic position now was more impregnable than ever. The company was producing close to two million pounds of copper a month, and the price hit an unbelievable thirty-two cents a pound by the fall of 1916. Up at the Mammoth mine two tunnels were driven a mile into the mountain to tap new ore bodies below the present working level. Heavy work was going forward on the company's outside properties as well.[31]

The Shasta County fruit crop fell far below normal in 1917. A dry winter, a long, hot summer, and the ravages of red spider were the excuses cited. Although the year had been difficult and discouraging, the county horticultural commissioner chirped, "We still have faith in this country and the coming of irrigation which we believe will do much to build up our resources." If there was any growling about smelter smoke the local newspapers declined to record it.

---

[31] *Redding Courier-Free Press*, January 14, April 20, May 10, 26, June 3, 1916; *Engineering and Mining Journal* 101 (1916), 201, 877.

Possibly the Shasta County farmers felt so thoroughly
crushed and intimidated by this time that they abandoned
all resistance. There is nothing to show that the Mammoth
company actually bothered to buy up the properties of the
more stiff-necked complainants, as happened around the
Selby and Anaconda smelters. More likely the company,
flush with war profits, had embarked on a program of en-
lightened profit sharing, quietly distributing "smoke payments" on a somewhat more generous scale.[32]

At least some of the farmers were able to supplement their
income by bearing arms for Mammoth that fall. The season
was a bad one for labor troubles all up and down the Pacific
coast, and the Shasta copper belt was one of the outstanding
hot spots. Mammoth's miners together with those of neighboring companies struck for three weeks in September 1917,
and affairs threatened to get ugly. Mammoth's management
let the cry go out that the difficulty was inspired by "agitators
who are enemies of the United States" and began "deputiz-
ing" local ranchers, sticking pistols and shotguns in their
hands. Simon Lubin of the California Commission of Immi-
gration and Housing happened to be in the area at the time
specifically looking for evidence of Wobbly incendiarism and
sabotage. He promptly denounced Mammoth Copper for its
bellicose and irresponsible tactics, telling the press the company had merely scraped up a gang of hired gunmen and had
been preparing to spill blood for its profit margin only.[33]

But surely after twenty years of squeezing and pressing, the
Shasta farmers were in no frame of mind to recognize any
common cause with diggers of copper, whether management

---

[32] *Redding Courier-Free Press*, September 4, 1917; Shasta County grantor and grantee
indexes, Shasta County Recorder's Office, Redding, Calif.; Hughes and Timpanogos Research Associates, "United States Smelting, Refining, and Mining Company Corporate
Records Inventory," 16, 134–35; Scott Miller (Arava Natural Resources Company, Helper,
Utah) to Khaled J. Bloom, September 9, 2003 (author's files).

[33] *Redding Courier-Free Press*, August 28, September 19, 1917.

or labor. And government commissions were giving them less reason all the time to think a renewed campaign against Mammoth could ever be successful. Back in 1913 the supervisors and district attorney of Solano County had finally wearied of their tedious struggle against the Selby smelter and agreed to submit the question of smoke injury around Benicia to an "expert commission," something that had been urged by Selby for a long time. It was stipulated in advance that this commission's conclusions and recommendations would be entered into the court record as modifications of the original 1906 injunction. This was done over the protests of Benicia people, who feared the investigation would be controlled by smelter sympathizers and amount to nothing but a "whitewash." They frantically appealed to state attorney general U. S. Webb to block the proceedings. Webb replied that he saw nothing irregular and refused to intervene.[34]

A whitewash was exactly what they got. The final report, over five hundred pages, was filed with the Solano County Superior Court at the end of 1914 and published the following year as Bulletin 98 of the U.S. Bureau of Mines. The opening pages of the report set the tone for the whole document: "The farmer, not familiar with technical or scientific matters, observing peculiar markings on his crops in the vicinity of a smelter, very naturally blames the smoke as the cause of trouble. . . . It is much easier for him to blame the smelter than it is to investigate carefully and learn positively the actual cause of the trouble which he sees." The subtleties of physical and organic chemistry and plant physiology were not matters upon which the poor yokels could be expected to have any competence, but leaving aside those whose views were "palpably colored by motives of cupidity," they still were teachable, and grateful for what they were taught. "When the average farmer has really become familiar with the subject,

---

[34] *Benicia Herald*, March 7, 21, 28, April 4, 11, 1913.

he is most reasonable and guarded in any statement he may make that 'smoke' is responsible for all his ills. With such an estimate of the usual intelligent citizen of this country, the commission has undertaken its labors in a spirit of helpfulness to both the farmers and the smelting company." The report of the Selby Smelter Commission is still saluted in some textbooks as a landmark in the scientific study of industrial air pollution. An original reading reveals a monument of patronizing circumlocution and learned obfuscation.[35]

A mineralogist from the bureau was designated a "legal agent," charged with interviewing a variety of Benicia people to determine whether an objective state of nuisance really existed. He concluded that it did not, "looking at things sanely and reasonably." The question, he decided, was largely a psychological one, involving prejudiced attitudes forged by more than ten years of "active agitation." He thought it probable that the fair-minded people of the community still were unconsciously swayed by the hard-headed and vociferous ones—farmers who smelled a rat or had an axe to grind—and thereby tricked themselves into believing as facts things that were "highly ludicrous and improbable, not to say impossible." "The agitation," he advised, "began with the farmers who have been the most bitter complainants all along, and who aroused the sympathies of the citizens with their declarations of inability to raise crops or to keep horses. The frequency with which horses died, some of them on the main business street of the town, together with the distressing blowing or roaring that was characteristic, did more to arouse the community to action than any other factor." Horses and cows still were getting sick, though maybe not in such large numbers, and the so-styled legal agent was inclined to think

[35] Holmes, Franklin, and Gould, *Report of the Selby Smelter Commission*, 10; Kenneth W. Nelson, Michael O. Varner, and Thomas J. Smith, "Nonferrous Metallurgical Operations," in Stern, *Air Pollution*, vol. 4, 847–48.

the real trouble was tuberculosis. He found plenty of human residents still complaining of throat and lung trouble and like ailments, but he thought this was precisely where psychology affected them. "So long as smoke is discharged from the stack, a great many people are going to continue to believe that harm is being done; if not visible harm or damage, then some insidious form of damage that will manifest itself after awhile"—a crank notion if there ever was one. It is worth noting that the Selby Smelter Commission's own chemical tests of the Benicia atmosphere showed that sulfur dioxide levels occasionally reached as high as seven parts per million, enough to make the most stalwart human subject cough. Its tests of dust collected on vaselined plates disclosed lead concentrations as high as 4,150 parts per million.[36]

A study of plant diseases and insect pests in the Benicia smoke zone was entrusted to J. W. Blankenship, Wyatt Jones, and R. W. Doane. Blankenship already was red-flagged in U.S. Department of Justice files as a "well-known professional witness" for the smelting industry—his effort to trace the withering of vegetation in Montana's Deerlodge Valley not to sulfur dioxide but to an indigenous "drying-up disease," which he claimed to have just discovered, was one of the more revolting incidents in the 1906 Anaconda smoke trial. More recently he had been involved in cooking up similar counterevidence for the Balaklala Copper Company, before it decided, for extrinsic commercial reasons, to throw in the towel in its controversy with the Shasta farmers. Jones and Doane had been doing work along the same lines for the Mammoth company. Blankenship and Jones's pathological survey concluded that the backward condition of vegetation around Benicia was traceable entirely to "plant diseases, predaceous insects, poor soil, poor cultivation, lack of water,

---

[36] Holmes, Franklin, and Gould, *Selby Smelter Commission*, 11–14, 181–88, 338–77.

and indifference to all of these conditions by the farmers of
the area"—and most emphatically, "not at all to smelter
smoke." They admitted finding evidence of sulfur dioxide injury in some of the coves directly across from the Selby
smelter, but insisted that this damage was "not general in any
sense but confined to a few places widely scattered." Widespread blotchings and mottlings on the farmers' barley and
oats were explained away as bacterial blight; the poor health
of their fruit trees was attributed to shothole and a variety of
other fungal diseases. Where those explanations fell short,
the thirty-square-mile smoke zone seems to have offered a
universal range of adverse climatic conditions to pick from—
drought here and waterlogging there; excessively foggy air in
one place and excessively arid winds in another.[37]

Doane's insect survey found twenty-five species of bugs
"doing more or less damage to plants of all kinds." He metic-
ulously cataloged the presence of scales and aphids, hoppers
and thrips, mites and borers—but neglected to specify to what
extent if any they affected the overall condition of crops. He
did pointedly criticize "slipshod methods of farming" and the
lack of proper pruning and spraying. Not one of the suspicious
farmers accepted his condescending offer to coach them on
how to control their pests, which he took to be further evidence of their laziness and perversity. A soil survey by University of California expert Charles Shaw served to show first
that the soils of the Benicia smoke zone were below par in
natural fertility, and second that they were not being poisoned
by any substances precipitated from Selby smelter smoke as
local farmers complained. Topsoil samples tested as high as
fifty parts per million of arsenic and twenty-two parts per million of lead, but this expert decided that "such quantities of

---

[37] Ibid., 47–50, 381–427; MacMillan, *Smoke Wars*, 118–20. See also Dillon, *Great Expectations*, 189.

arsenic and lead have no adverse influence on the growth of
plants, indeed such small quantities seem rather to stimulate
their growth." A veterinary survey headed by C. M. Haring,
another elastic luminary of the state university, allowed that
numerous horses had suffered from lead and arsenic poisoning
in past years but concluded that recent improvements at the
Selby smelter had eliminated "all possibility" of future mischief. Among the professional consultants helping Haring to
this conclusion were Dr. Veramus Moore of Cornell University and Dr. H. C. Gardiner of Montana, both of whom had
been instrumental in preparing Amalgamated Copper's defense in the Anaconda smoke trial.[38]

"We congratulate all concerned on the findings of this
commission," the *Mining and Scientific Press* said. "It has set
standards for others and has solved problems that were leading to endless bitterness and litigation." But around the Penn
smelter at Campo Seco in Calaveras County there was still
plenty of bitterness and a glut of litigation too. In the spring
of 1915, thirty-five farmers and ranchers from the surrounding foothills filed individual suits for damages against the
Penn company totaling $334,000. Their depositions recited
the same old story. For years they had watched the orbit of
ruin widening and lodged futile complaints with the Penn
management. Repeated appeals to county officials brought
no satisfaction. They told how the "copper smoke" drifted

[38] Holmes, Franklin, and Gould, *Selby Smelter Commission*, 50–55, 428–67, 474–502;
MacMillan, *Smoke Wars*, 113–18. In fact, horse deaths linked to lead poisoning would
continue to crop up in the Benicia area for many years: a particularly bad episode was described in the *Journal of the American Veterinary Association* in 1953. The loss of a herd of
prize Appaloosas in 1969 prompted a major study by the state health department, which
found that continuing smelter-fumes pollution had made Benicia and its environs an "unhealthy place in which to live." Citing cheap foreign competition, American Smelting
and Refining permanently closed the Selby smelter soon after: see *San Francisco Chronicle*,
March 8, June 2, July 28, 1970; *Benicia Herald*, June 3, 1970, March 17, 1971; California
Air Resources Board, "A Joint Study of Lead Contamination Relative to Horse Deaths in
Southern Solano County."

along the gulches and gathered in the vales which were the most valuable parts of their properties. They recognized that it was most potent when it came up mixed with fog—they knew it by smell and taste; some nights it was strong enough to wake them up choking and sneezing. Fence wires and window screens bore a "mildewed" appearance after a heavy smoking and rusted through in no time. Their barley crops were down more than half, so was the carrying capacity of their pastures, and the almond orchards many of them had set out years before were withering away and frequently lost blossoms and nutlets to smoke visitations. One farmer claimed to have lost a thousand-dollar almond crop when the smoke rolled in thick one spring night. "If the farmers should go to the smelter and do a thousand dollars worth of vandalism in one night, what would happen?" he asked, shrewdly or naively. The Penn ore evidently carried considerable arsenic as well as sulfur, and the ranchers had lost numerous cattle to what they called "inflamed stomach." Some claimed they were unable to clear a dollar a day under present conditions and wanted to leave the district, but when they tried to move away had been advised by realtors that their places were unsalable. Penn, a Standard Oil subsidiary, answered that its smoke was blameless and that the plaintiffs' farms were simply worn out. All cases were dismissed by the U.S. district court in September 1916. To hammer the lesson home, the farmers were held for the company's costs of court. George Baker, last holdout among the Shasta farmers, dropped his personal suit for damages against Mammoth the very next day.[39]

[39] *Mining and Scientific Press* 109 (1914), 939; *Engineering and Mining Journal* 99 (1915), 424; 100 (1915), 244; 102 (1916), 70, 607; Civil Case Files 15798, 15818, 15820, and 15837, and Equity Case Files 250 and 251, U.S. District Court for the Northern District of California, Record Group 21, National Archives and Records Administration–Pacific Region (San Francisco), San Bruno, Calif.

"Smoke farming appears to have been abated as a department of agriculture," the *Engineering and Mining Journal* snig-
gered in 1917, in its review of "The Year's Progress in
Metallurgy." Indeed, antismelter activity was having hard
sledding everywhere about this time. The exigencies of war
production and the swelling wealth and political muscle of
the metallurgical and chemical industries appear to have fortified beyond measure the attitude that there were "certain
circumstances" where the customary rights of individuals
could not be maintained in opposition to "the good of the
community." The farmers and stockmen of Yavapai County,
Arizona, organized against the United Verde smelter at
Jerome in 1916; when the issue finally was concluded in 1921
the state court awarded the complainants one dollar each for
their losses. A similar movement against Phelps Dodge by
the ranchers of Cochise County, Arizona, fell apart without
bringing suit at all. In Ontario, Canada, the courts had settled on a policy of flatly refusing the injunction to complaining farmers and restricting them to recovery of damages.
The provincial legislature formalized this in 1921 with an
act that required binding arbitration instead of litigation in
smelter-smoke controversies. In the first batch of settlements
concluded under this law, damage claims totaling $20,000
against International Nickel at Sudbury were knocked down
to just $925. In Utah, the 1909 accord that had been used as
the model for the Shasta farmers' 1910 agreement with
Mammoth had likewise turned out rather badly for the complainants, and in 1919 Salt Lake County farmers petitioned
the federal district court for a new order. Judge Tillman Johnson withheld it, observing that the farmers' chronic "nervous
irritation" and ingrained "mental attitude" made it impossible to tell whether an objective state of nuisance really existed. "It would seem that so-called Christian Science ought

to be an effective preventive for the latter trouble," the *Mining and Scientific Press* wisecracked.[40]

But the Great War turned out to be both zenith and finale for the Mammoth Copper Company and its operations in Shasta County, California. Reserves proved to be dwindling as vigorous exploration work failed to open new ore bodies large enough to replace the quantities mined. Prices collapsed when the sudden contraction of industry after the armistice left buyers and sellers with huge inventories of copper on their hands—by the winter of 1918 there was hardly any market for the stuff at all. Mammoth turned out a million pounds of red metal as late as February 1919 and was reported to be hoping for improved conditions by summer, but the operation admittedly was skating on a ragged edge. A wage dispute that May occasioned a walkout, which furnished an excuse for drawing the furnace fires and closing the plant down—permanently, as it turned out. The smelter hardware was sold for scrap in 1926 and the city of Kennett was officially disincorporated a few years later. By 1941, as the waters of Shasta Reservoir rose to blot it out forever, nothing remained of the former boomtown but a block or two of crumbling brick buildings.[41]

[40] *Engineering and Mining Journal* 103 (1917), 53, 514, 1038, 112 (1921), 632, 913, 114 (1922), 72; *Mining and Scientific Press* 120 (1920), 854. The same winds of war blew away twenty or thirty years of progress in coal-smoke abatement in many eastern cities: see Stradling, *Smokestacks and Progressives*, 147–50.

[41]. *Redding Courier-Free Press*, May 7, 12, 15–16, 1919; *San Francisco Chronicle*, February 5, 1926; April 15, 1930; February 25, 1941.

CHAPTER FIVE

"A picture of woeful and absolute desolation"

The federal government did not altogether abandon interest in the Shasta County smoke situation after settling its case with the Mountain Copper Company in May 1908. It recognized that conditions around Keswick would have to be checked from time to time so any further injuries could be identified and dealt with. It also sensed an approaching confrontation with the new smelters that were coming into production up the canyon from Keswick. That summer a Department of Justice agent visited the area in company with John Haywood of the Bureau of Chemistry and a representative of the Forest Service. The Mammoth Copper Company had been smelting at Kennett for almost three years, and Balaklala's big ore-reduction plant at Coram was about to start up. The government men were disturbed to find that an additional eight-by-ten-mile strip along the Sacramento canyon already had been desolated, "just as complete as it is around the Keswick smelter." Even the manzanita bushes, the toughest of the local species, had been killed out. The tributary valleys to a distance of five miles from Kennett were filled with thousands of dead or dying trees, "the forest practically entirely destroyed."[1]

---

[1] W. J. Hughes to solicitor general, August 19, 1908, in DOJ 5706–1898.

The experts were sure that an excellent case could be made against the new smelter, but they were en route to study a similar problem at Anaconda, Montana, and decided that further investigation would have to be put off until the following year. An abundance of rainy weather and southerly winds that winter spread fume damage northward and east-ward to an alarming extent. Poisonous smoke was blown far up the valleys of the Pit and McCloud rivers. The superintendent of the Shasta National Forest reported that the fringes of the reserve, seven miles north of the smelter, had been affected. The superintendent of the U.S. Fishery Station at Baird, on the McCloud River eight miles above Kennett, advised his superiors that all the trees on the reservation would be killed unless something was done soon. "A thousand dead trees can be seen from the porch of the dwelling, and it is supposed that the orchard, as well as the oak and pine, will be killed." Forest Service rangers confirmed that the mature growth of ponderosa pines had been severely damaged over a wide area, while seedling growth appeared to have been completely killed. This troubling news moved the commissioner of the General Land Office to order a comprehensive review of the situation. Paul M. Paine, a forest engineer with the agency, was assigned to undertake the study.[2]

In the fall of 1909 Paine spent most of a month examining public lands in the region. He took care to distinguish between tracts where vegetation had been entirely wiped out and those where the native trees and shrubs had been "sickened" but not "devastated." The frequent brush fires the

[2] F. E. Olmstead to forester, February 2, 1909, commissioner of Bureau of Fisheries to chief of Bureau of Forestry, March 9, 1909, and L. N. Lorenzen to W. B. Rider, March 27, 1909, in FS RCF; chief of field service of General Land Office to O. W. Lange, April 14, 1909, in GLO 55979. It is important to note that the southern boundary of the Shasta National Forest was then about seven miles south of its present location; see U.S. Congress, *Hearings before a Subcommittee of the Committee on Interior and Insular Affairs.*

smoke zone was prone to unfortunately had "vitiated the evidence as to what is strictly due to fumes." In addition, Paine found that the different local species varied considerably in their susceptibility to smelter smoke, the coniferous trees apparently very sensitive, while the manzanita and poison oak underbrush seemed rather tolerant. The zone in which vegetation had been entirely destroyed was still comparatively limited, confined for the most part to the Sacramento canyon below Kennett. Of the tributary watersheds, the valley of Big Backbone Creek, leading directly up into the national forest from the Mammoth smelter, exhibited by far the greatest degree of unquestionable smoke injury. Paine did not say devastation here was total at that time, but most of this land certainly would graduate to that status over the next few years.

"The area in which the sickness of timber is apparent covers, of course, a much wider extent of territory," Paine observed. This anomalous sickness, showing mainly on the pines, extended along both flanks of the Sacramento canyon as far as Gregory, ten miles north of Kennett—right about where today Interstate Highway 5 crosses the Shasta Reservoir lakehead. West of Kennett the smoke was confined by the high ridge which separates the watersheds of the Sacramento and Trinity rivers, but eastward it could follow the natural corridor furnished by the valleys of the Pit and Mc-Cloud rivers, whose waters flowed into the Sacramento just above Kennett. The "sickness of timber" reached up the Pit River as far as fourteen miles and could be traced almost as far up the McCloud, fading away several miles beyond Baird. Southeast of Kennett, severe smoke damage was evident at least as far as the Buckeye-Baird road—approximately the route Interstate 5 takes as it swings around Shasta Reservoir. This encompassed a wide circle of territory indeed. Including the smoke-blighted farm and ranch country below Redding, which Paine did not survey, it would not be extravagant to say that one thousand square miles of land were being adversely impacted by smelter fumes. The Balaklala and Mammoth smelters both were running full blast by this time. Sulfur dioxide releases were at a peak, and farmers and ranchers in the country below were organizing for a fight.[3]

Paine's assessments concerned only tangible injury to vegetation, and he did not try to evaluate less evident effects on the health of the native woodlands. Later smelter-fume studies conducted by the U.S. Department of Agriculture in Washington State and Montana would show that sulfur dioxide sharply retards the height and diameter growth of conifers even where lesions on the foliage are slight or absent. The gas also has a severe effect on natural reproduction and restocking, causing reduced cone crops as well as increased seedling mortality. And such effects doubtless extended over a much larger area than Paine imagined. A tree-ring study published in the journal *Science* in 1984 revealed that the growth of pines in the Great Smoky Mountains National Park had been suppressed markedly during the years of heavy copper smelting at Ducktown, Tennessee. This timber was more than fifty miles downwind from Ducktown; contemporary investigators had traced visible injury only thirteen miles in that direction.[4]

But most of the land of any real value in the Kennett smoke zone already had passed into private hands, Paine discovered. Outside the national forest only 15,077 acres remained in federal ownership, generally consisting of "steep mountain slopes, burnt-over areas, and odd isolated tracts

<hr>

[3] Paul M. Paine to commissioner of General Land Office, October 30, 1909, 10–21, in GLO 55979.

[4] Scheffer and Hedgcock, *Injury to Northwestern Forest Trees by Sulfur Dioxide from Smelters*; Baer and McLaughlin, "Trace Elements in Tree Rings," 494–97; Haywood, *Injury to Vegetation and Animal Life by Smelter Wastes*, 15–21.

with no bodies of merchantable timber. Most of it, however, is covered with a more or less heavy growth of underbrush, much of which either has been, or may be, killed by the fumes and the land brought towards the condition of that surrounding the old Keswick smelter." Paine thought that substantial damage could be proved surely enough, at least on the 4,880 acres where all vegetation had been completely killed, and that the value of this damage could be recovered surely enough in court. "In view of the well-known principle of small timber and brush preventing erosion and holding back moisture in the ground during the flood season till the later, dry period, it is believed the courts would recognize the value of such lands, even where they have held no large commercial timber." However, he pointed out that there was no guide for placing a definite value on such land, "other than that the Government has placed itself on record, in the sale of isolated tracts, timber and stone entries, and in connection with the original California and Oregon Railroad grant, as considering that the land has a minimum value of $2.50 an acre." (Ultimately the government would settle for not quite forty cents an acre.)

Whether smelter-fumes injury would extend beyond its present limits could not be determined without a second examination at a later date, Paine said. "My own belief is that such will be found to be true, unless the smelters discover a remedy." Unfortunately, no workable scheme for doing away with the smoke was in sight. He explained the various drawbacks of acid manufacture and other proposed solutions. Confronted with a stop-work injunction, the smelters could invoke a number of considerations in their defense: the importance of their product and their payrolls, the taxes they paid, and the fact that a whole county's "growth and prosperity" depended on their operation. And, Paine cautioned, a defense along those lines had proved effective in a number

of previous cases, notably that of the United States versus
the Mountain Copper Company. There were also certain political repercussions to be considered—what he called "the
local situation." He concluded that injunction proceedings
would be "very ill-advised, both because of the material interests that would be affected and the public feeling that
would be engendered, especially towards the Forest Service,
in the event of such action."[5]

The "undesirable political aspect" that might attend rash
or hasty litigation was even more of a consideration in a case
the government was then preparing against an Anaconda,
Montana, smelter whose smoke was crippling timber on surrounding national forest lands, besides killing cattle and crops
on farms in the adjacent Deerlodge Valley. For all its environmental ravages, the giant Washoe copper plant at Anaconda
was deemed a marvel of contemporary technology and one of
the brightest stars of American industry. It was the biggest
smelter in the world, pouring out more than 100 million
pounds of copper a year, 20 percent of the nation's supply. It
was far and away the biggest industrial concern in Montana,
exercising near-total control over the state's politics and jour-
nalism. Linked financially to Standard Oil and the House of
Morgan, it enjoyed abundant pull in national politics as well.
"A commercial Hercules," one of the government's attorneys
called it. The Justice Department understandably quailed at
the prospect of tackling such a Hercules head on. It determined to take its time and prepare its case with utmost cau-
tion. Thick reports and much correspondence followed. There
were careful chemical and botanical investigations of the character and extent of smoke injury, painstaking technical and
commercial studies of acid manufacture and other possible
remedies. A comprehensive suit for injunction was framed,

[5] Paul M. Paine to commissioner of General Land Office, October 30, 1909, 21–29, in
GLO 55979.

drafted, refined. Field, laboratory, and office work on this case would drag along until 1911.[6]

During this interim the federal government was not inattentive to the smoke problem in California. In the spring of 1910 the Justice Department sent a special agent out to negotiate with the Shasta County smelters, after drawing up bills for injunction signed by the attorney general to hold ready in case they would not come to terms. The companies, simultaneously trying to stave off parallel action by the Shasta County Farmers' Protective Association, on the contrary seemed to be "exceedingly anxious to avoid litigation." They disclosed their plans to abate their smoke, Balaklala with its electrical precipitation plant and Mammoth with its baghouse. "The companies understood that the Government did not accept these appliances in satisfaction of its demand, but merely that the Government would delay action until the efficiency of the appliances was demonstrated." The smelters began installing the proposed devices and the government suspended further action. Local people were not informed of the proceedings contemplated by the government, or of the understanding it finally reached with the companies. A small copper smelter recently started up on the Pit River by the General Electric corporation took this opportunity to close down, the company stating, "confidentially, that they were perfectly willing to close if any excuse for closing could be offered and that they preferred to do this, inasmuch as they were making nothing under their then operations."[7]

Meanwhile, the U.S. Forest Service had been requested to organize field and laboratory investigations of the smelter-fumes problem. "If the matter is litigated we will need all the expert testimony available as cases of this character are very

[6] MacMillan, *Smoke Wars*, 145–210.

[7] Ligon Johnson to attorney general, November 8, 1911, and May 20, 1913, and W. R. Harr to John E. Raker, September 3, 1912, in DOJ 144276; *Redding Courier-Free Press*, May 31, 1910.

bitterly fought." The government recognized that obfuscation was the companies' most potent defensive weapon in
lawsuits of this type, as industry journalists even then were
blatantly proclaiming: "It is only necessary to show that there
are other causes than smoke playing a large part and the burden of proof immediately falls upon the prosecution to show
how much of the damage has actually been done by the
smoke, and unless he can accomplish this his case at once
falls to pieces." To defeat the injunction suit brought against
it by the Deerlodge County, Montana, farmers three years
before, the Anaconda smelter had imported a troop of well-
compensated Ivy League experts led by Harvard's Theobald
Smith to massage its rebutting evidence into plausible shape.
The transcript of testimony in the hard-fought case filled
sixty-three printed volumes; for sheer bulk it was thought to
have set a record in American judicial history.[8]

Obfuscation was a successful counterstrategy in the court-
room largely because scientific information about sulfur dioxide and its effects was so imperfect. Professor George J.
Peirce, plant physiologist of Stanford University, was engaged by the Forest Service to experiment with the effects
of very dilute doses of sulfur dioxide on young trees. If the
minimum dose that did harm could be determined experi-
mentally, the government men reasoned, then air analysis
revealing more than that amount in the smoke zone would
establish a plain cause-and-effect relationship, "and no
amount of argument or denial on the part of the smeltermen
can change the fact." One of the interesting results Peirce
obtained was that pine seedlings grown in clean air made
considerably better growth than seedlings exposed intermit-

    [8] Burton and Reed, "Smelter Fumes and Damage Suits," 211–12; Ligon Johnson to as-
sistant forester, April 12, 1909, in FS RCF; *Butte (Mont.) Inter Mountain*, March 28, 1907;
Civil Case File 1738, Ninth U.S. Circuit Court of Appeals, Record Group 276, National
Archives and Records Administration–Pacific Region (San Francisco), San Bruno, Calif.

tently to wee concentrations of the gas, insufficient to cause visible injury.[9]

In August 1910 the Justice Department sent John Haywood back west to review conditions around Kennett. He was accompanied by J. D. Coffman, a silviculturist detailed by the Forest Service. The investigators spent four days tramping up and down the denuded canyon of the Sacramento and the desolated basins of Squaw and Big and Little Backbone creeks. From ridge to ridge in the canyon, and for a distance of four or five miles up the creeks, the killing of vegetation ranged from "practically complete" to "absolute." The only species able to persist outside of a few sheltered ravines was poison oak. "Stumps, clumps of dead brush, or standing or fallen dead timber are all that remain to indicate the former forest cover." For miles beyond that zone the damage was only relatively less severe. Coffman's assignment was to determine how much if any of the destruction possibly could be ascribed to wildfires, plant pests and diseases, or other causes than smelter fumes. He concluded that sulfur dioxide was the only pathological agent that could account for the total killing of all plant species and the total absence of any signs of regeneration.[10]

And yet Coffman was satisfied that most of the land affected was private land, and damage to timber in the Shasta National Forest itself was not very extensive or severe—so far. This was in accord with Haywood's observations. The investigators were of the opinion that smoke injury in the region would probably increase and spread, however. Neither the baghouse nor the Cottrell apparatus would alleviate the problem, they forecast, because neither process would do anything to eliminate the sulfur dioxide, "and it is this gas which

[9] F. E. Olmstead to forester, May 26, 1910, in FS RCF.
[10] J. D. Coffman to R. F. Hammatt, September 26, 1910, in FS RCF.

is killing and injuring the vegetation." Professor Peirce of
Stanford also predicted that the new smoke-eating devices
would be ineffective, feeling that they had been installed
merely "to pacify the farmers of the vicinity for a short time."
The district forester in San Francisco strongly urged that
Peirce be authorized to extend his studies to include actual
field conditions in Shasta County. "It is quite evident that we
are going to have this smelter nuisance to contend with for
some years to come and that we should take all possible steps
toward securing information regarding this matter." But the
Forest Service deferred to the Justice Department, which was
coming to its own very different conclusion on the matter.[11]

   "It has taken considerable expense not only in the matter
of first cost but also in alterations and adjustments to bring
the bag house to its present state of perfection," Department
of Justice special assistant Ligon Johnson informed the U.S.
attorney general's office in November 1911. Mammoth's
smoke was being filtered, neutralized, and diluted as per
agreement, Johnson reported, and there already were signs
that new vegetation was beginning to reclothe the nearby
hills. His incredible conclusion: "There is no question as to
improvement of conditions by the bag house. . . . There is
no trace of injury this year upon Government lands and so
far as the United States are concerned, unless there should be
some unexpected change, all injury and fear of injury by the
Mammoth company has been completely eliminated." A
subsequent report stated that nothing remained to be settled
but the question of compensation for damages inflicted prior
to installation of the baghouse. This was certainly contrary
to the situation reported by the California Smelter Wastes
Commission a few years later. Standing on a ridge above
Kennett in the spring of 1914, James McMurphy of the Stan-

---

[11] Acting chief of Bureau of Chemistry to R. S. Graves, October 15, 1910, and acting
assistant forester to district forester, July 18, 1910, in FS RCF.

ford botany department considered the miles of barren waste around him to be "all the evidence needed to convince one" that Mammoth's emissions still were suppressing and destroying vegetation. On the outskirts of the barren area Mc-Murphy found the native shrubs and trees "so badly damaged that I cannot understand how they could remain alive if the smelter did much more damage in the years before the baghouse was put in than in the present season."[12]

But the Department of Justice evidently wanted a seemly excuse to back away from the impending showdown. No doubt the department was disheartened by the failure of the Montana farmers' appeal in the Ninth U.S. Circuit Court of Appeals in March 1911. The opinion was delivered by Erskine Ross, the same judge who had downed the U.S. government's case against the Mountain Copper Company five years before. Ross was firm as ever in his theory that the power to enjoin an important industry rested entirely with the sound discretion of the court and that those affected by a nuisance emanating from such an industry could not demand its abatement as an absolute right. He agreed with the trial judge's finding that injuries to the farmers' lands were "very slight" compared to the general distress that would follow the closing of the Anaconda smelter. It was a judge's responsibility, he repeated, "to consider all the facts and circumstances of the case in order to determine the equities," and to refuse the injunction "where it appears that it will necessarily operate contrary to the real justice of the case." The Justice Department obviously recognized that any action it might bring was bound to end up in this same court,

[12] Ligon Johnson to attorney general, November 8, 1911, and September 25, 1912, in DOJ 144276; James McMurphy, "A Report to the Smelter Wastes Commission on the Botanical Investigation of Injury to Vegetation by Smelter Wastes in the Vicinity of Redding, Calif.," in "Affidavit Showing Reasonable Necessity for the Examination and Inspection of Defendant's Smelter and the Operations Thereof," December 1, 1914, in NDC 15122.

likely on the lap of this same judge. Without litigation, the government moved to settle its case against the Anaconda smelter a few weeks after the decision in the Montana farmers' suit was handed down. Apparently it made the decision to compromise its dispute with the California smelters as well.[13]

In March 1912 the Interior Department called the Justice Department's attention to the fact that action on Paul Paine's report on the Kennett smelter area had been held in abeyance for over two years. Attorney General George Wickersham explained that his department had been and still was absorbed in other cases. He advised that any legal proceedings be deferred until the fall and suggested that in the meantime a resurvey be made of smelter-fume injuries in Shasta County, to establish the amount of damages and determine whether there had been any aggravation of the situation. One of the timber cruisers of the General Land Office's field division was assigned to make the investigation, visiting Shasta County in August 1912 and again in October of that year. J. B. Chatterton was instructed to report on damages to standing timber, both stumpage and cordwood values, also on the damage to seedling and sapling growth, as well as any damage from soil erosion, whether in the mountains or on the valley lands below.[14]

Chatterton concluded that prevailing wind patterns had kept serious fume damage from extending more than six or seven miles north of Kennett, although it could be traced southward as far as thirty-five miles. He thought further injury to vegetation in the Sacramento canyon would be lim-

[13] "Bliss v. Washoe Copper Co. et al.," 824; MacMillan, *Smoke Wars*, 211–15. See also Frederick, *Rugged Justice*, 98–121.

[14] Assistant secretary of interior to attorney general, March 12, 1912, attorney general to secretary of interior, March 12, 1912, commissioner of General Land Office to F. C. Dezendorf, March 20, 1912, and assistant chief of field service of General Land Office to F. C. Dezendorf, September 26, 1912, in GLO 55979.

ited for another reason: the plain, sorry fact that everything within reach of the smoke was already completely destroyed. Chatterton said conditions in the vicinity of Kennett appeared to be about the same as Paine described them in 1909, except that many of the dead trees had since toppled over or burned down. Here again, his appraisal of fume damage was complicated by the fact that much of the land had been swept by wildfires. He identified a couple of tracts of unclaimed government land that might have been suitable for farming and fruit raising, "but," in the terse language of his notes, "not possible under present conditions; land poisoned (residents say) by arsenic fumes from Kennett smelter." Virtually all the old ranches and homesteads in and around the canyon had been abandoned long before. Chatterton found a few spots that showed "prospects of reviving growth of brush and small oak," but for the most part the damage to forest reproduction appeared to be absolute. "There is no evidence of revival on the lands reported. Damage to vegetation in general and damage by erosion of soil is evidenced by gullies on hills and deposit of silt in gulches. This is very marked in comparison with tracts on which vegetation is living." But so far, he said, not too much of this sediment had drifted beyond the gulches, and people in the country below were not complaining of its effects.

Chatterton examined 6,440 acres of public land in the smoke zone and submitted an itemized statement of timber losses. He fixed total damages at $3,783.75, including 1,253 cords of fuel wood at an average price of fifty-eight cents a cord and 9,597 feet of mine props at two cents a foot. "The values placed are the going prices for these timber products in this country," he assured his superiors. His estimate did not cover soil erosion losses, nor did it make any allowance for the devastation of young growth, for the cost of artificial reforestation, or for destruction of the land's market value.

Furthermore, only the two townships immediately north and south of Kennett had been surveyed; left out entirely were three townships to the east where Paul Paine had found serious damage in 1909. Chatterton did not say whether he regarded his figure as full or adequate compensation to the American public, but it was on the basis of that sum that the American government proceeded to settle.[15]

After a fifteen-year war of attrition against the California smelters, the federal government evidently was in a mood not just to compromise but to capitulate. There is no hint in the records that an injunction suit or any other legal action was considered at this time. "I believe without litigation I could secure $3,000 in settlement," the Justice Department's special assistant stated as he headed west the following April to negotiate. Several conversations with Mammoth's attorney extracted a written offer that "for purposes of compromise, and without any admission of liability, the company will pay the Government $2,500 in full settlement of its claim." Special Assistant Johnson recommended that the offer be accepted. He pointed out that Mammoth was not properly chargeable with the whole amount of timber destruction in the area, while the Balaklala plant, also culpable, was closed now and practically abandoned. The chief of the General Land Office's San Francisco field office agreed that the offer was "a fair and equitable one." The Department of the Interior approved the deal in June 1913, and the transaction was consummated in August.[16]

Mammoth had every reason to congratulate itself on the

[15] J. B. Chatterton to commissioner of General Land Office, August 25 and November 13, 1912, in GLO 55979.

[16] Ligon Johnson to commissioner of General Land Office, April 3, 1913, Alfred Sutro to Ligon Johnson, May 12, 1913, Ligon Johnson to attorney general, May 20, 1913, F. C. Dezendorf to commissioner of General Land Office, May 22, 1913, assistant secretary of interior to attorney general, June 24, 1913, and assistant solicitor of treasury to commissioner of General Land Office, August 8, 1913, in GLO 55979.

outcome. It had relieved itself of the threat of federal interference and virtually was at liberty to do as it pleased, all for
a very modest consideration in relation to its ability to pay.
The Kennett plant had poured out over $4 million in copper
in 1912. Its parent company in Boston recorded net earnings
of almost $4 million that year, paying a dividend of 7 per-
cent to holders of its preferred stock. Why the U.S. government should have been satisfied with the settlement is less
clear. It had asserted no charge at all for loss of topsoil or the
cost of reforestation, but had been content to accept a nominal sum for stumpage and cordwood values, calculated after
nearly all the good timber already had been chopped down
or consumed by fire. The out-of-court deal completely ignored a long-standing California statute that prescribed tre-
ble damages for "wrongful injuries to timber, trees, or
undergrowth upon the land of another."[17]

All along the government had kept its investigations and
negotiations strictly confidential, and the fact that it had
reached a final settlement with Mammoth never was made
public. Querulous farmers down in the valley still were writing to various departments in Washington, trying to rouse
an apparently indifferent or absentminded government to
the fact that public lands as well as their own were being devastated. From his family's place near Redding, Chum Gibson
informed the Department of Justice that fresh sections of the
Shasta National Forest were being injured, forwarding a par-
cel of shriveled leaves to illustrate the smelter's "good works
in the present season." He warned that the baghouse at Kennett was "as practical for controlling sulphur fumes as a sieve,
and the damage is going merrily on." The frustrated rancher
had gotten evasive replies to previous letters, and his tone

---

[17] *Engineering and Mining Journal* 93 (1912), 683; Deering, *The Civil Code of the State of
California*, 714–15.

by this time was bitter and impudent. "In conclusion," he scolded the U.S. attorney general, "I wish to say to you personally, if you are a man who is honest and not a grafter, not afraid to do your duty, you had better get experts into the National reserve where the injury is now being done, and make the Mammoth Company control its smoke, or within a year or two there will be no need of any (in)action on your part." Gibson's complaint was referred to Special Assistant Johnson, who advised only this: "I judge the smelters have declined to permit any blackmail to be levied upon them and Gibson is now trying to use the United States Government as a club in his operations. . . . I do not think that he is entitled to the courtesy of any reply." And accordingly no reply was given.[18]

In July 1913 the Balaklala company came forward with an offer to pony up $1,250. Higher copper prices were tempting the company to recommission its smelter at Coram. It was dickering with the Shasta County Farmers' Protective Association for formal permission to resume operations and obviously was eager to seize this opportunity to unburden itself of any complications with the federal government. The government was just as anxious to conclude matters, and the offer was speedily approved and accepted. There is no reason to think the final settlement presented any greater hardship to the Balaklala company than it had to Mammoth. By now Balaklala was a full subsidiary of American Smelters Securities, the Guggenheims' giant holding company, capitalized at $77 million. Shortly afterward, Special Assistant Johnson was ensconced in a Manhattan office as top "smoke counsel" for the Guggenheims, at double the salary the Justice Department had been paying him. At a conference in St. Louis in 1917, an audience of investors would hear him rem-

---

[18] Chum Gibson to W. R. Harr, November 11, 1912, and Ligon Johnson to attorney general, November 23, 1912, in DOJ 144276.

inisce about the trouble once posed by "communities of smoke farmers" whose idea of good husbandry was "to let their places grow up in weeds and collect from the smeltery the value of the maximum crops ever produced." "The price of peace was rising above the possible profits of smelting operations," he assured his appreciative listeners.[19]

So for a total of $3,750 the two companies had purchased the privilege of irreparably devastating thousands of acres of public land. By any standard of reckoning it was a bargain—ridiculously so. For damage to a smaller and inherently less valuable section of public domain the Mountain Copper Company had been required to tender an equivalent acreage of good forest land, plus $10,000 cash. But any additional sum the government could have extracted from the corporations at this time probably would have been about as insignificant over the long term—several times the money still would have been a paltry advance on the millions Uncle Sam spent on reclamation and reforestation here in later years. Whatever its real belief and intent, in January 1914 the U.S. General Land Office informed its San Francisco field office that it was closing the file on the Shasta County smelters. That summer came the Great War, and world demand for copper surged mightily. The Mammoth plant boosted its production of copper 60 percent by 1916, and it is reasonable to assume that its releases of sulfur dioxide rose in full proportion.[20]

The copper men had gotten just what they wanted out of the government. They got what they wanted out of the earth too, but a flayed and decomposing carcass was rather incon-

---

[19] Ligon Johnson to attorney general, July 8, 1913, assistant attorney general to secretary of interior, July 15, 1913, and Ligon Johnson to attorney general, February 11, 1914, in DOJ 144276; Johnson, "History and Legal Phases of the Smelting-Smoke Problem—II," 924.

[20] Assistant commissioner of General Land Office to F. C. Dezendorf, January 10, 1914, in GLO 55979; *Engineering and Mining Journal* 101 (1916), 201, 241, 1063.

veniently left behind. In 1919 Herbert Lang acknowledged "a secondary effect of some importance." "Divested of its protective covering of trees, brush, and herbage, the blanket of loose soil, unprotected from the storms of winter, has become furrowed by thousands of little watercourses, like wrinkles on the countenance of age." Agriculturally considered this soil never could have been of much value, Lang remarked, "but it is rather a pity that it should be lost." "Nature," he shrugged, "will doubtless take her own method of repairing these slight ravages, helped perhaps by some well considered scheme of scientific re-forestation."[21]

People who knew that locality must have chuckled at the writer's decided talent for understatement. The steady wasting of the smelter-denuded hills under the yearly attack of heavy rains had been observed for a long time, of course, and the practical consequences of massive soil erosion had been recognized at least since 1905, when a sudden landslide above Keswick shoved a Southern Pacific southbound completely off the track. An exceptionally intense spring storm in 1915 deluged the Sacramento canyon and the runoff poured down the naked slopes "as it would off the roof of a barn." The railroad suffered fifteen major mud-rock avalanches in the smelter area, with numerous culverts and one big trestle demolished, and for three weeks traffic between San Francisco and Portland had to be detoured through Nevada. A bad storm in the fall of 1918 knocked out both river bridges at Keswick and produced nine big slides in as many miles between there and Coram.[22]

Even in fair weather travelers on the railroad must have had certain melancholy reflections as they rolled through the barren gorge and looked up at its sterile, glaring slopes. The

---

[21] Lang, "A Metallurgical Journey to Shasta, California—V," 397–98.

[22] *Redding Courier-Free Press*, May 10–11, 1915; October 2–3, 1918; *Redding Searchlight*, March 29, 1907; *San Francisco Examiner*, May 12, 14, 1915.

watershed specialist Edward N. Munns surveyed the Kennett
smelter area for the California Board of Forestry in 1922 and
recorded his visual, not to say emotional, impressions of the
devastated canyon:

> From the Sacramento River on one hand to practically the sum-
> mit of the hills on either side, the land is devoid of cover as a high-
> way and the soil exposed to the action of the elements year in and
> year out. The hills are everywhere cut and gashed by the long fur-
> rows which run from practically the top of the hills to the bottom
> in straight lines, growing deeper and wider as they near the water-
> courses, which formerly were forest-lined, and now are gravel
> washes in the summer and torrents during the winter. The gullied
> hillsides, the barren slopes reflecting the tremendous summer heat,
> the gaunt naked skeletons of the former forest, the rock-filled
> channels and muddy water, combine with the poison oak that ap-
> parently was least injured by the fumes to give a picture of woeful
> and absolute desolation that only needs a buzzard and rattlesnake
> or howling coyote to complete it.

Munns's survey found 105 square miles of once-wooded
hills to be in an almost completely barren state, rain-washed,
sun-scorched, wholly forlorn. Enclosing that was another 135
square miles where the vegetation cover was horribly impaired but still clung to life to some slim degree. Munns's plot
measurements indicated that sheet and gully erosion already
had stripped at least 35 million cubic yards of earth from
these hills. At Nevada County's Malakoff Diggings, California's most notorious hydraulic mine, ten years of deliberate,
round-the-clock attack with billions of gallons of pressurized
water had managed to excavate only 25 million cubic yards.
Munns estimated continuing soil losses in the Shasta County
smelter area to be on the order of 350,000 cubic yards a year.
He had the opportunity to contrast storm runoff from Squaw
Creek basin, completely denuded, with that from a nearby
watershed where a healthy brush and timber cover was still
intact. "Squaw Creek water was muddy, violently muddy and

murky, and absolutely repulsive to the eye, and the material in it gritted one's teeth when tasted." Runoff from the forested area was scarcely tinted: "The water was discolored, chiefly from floating and suspended vegetable matter, but it cleared much sooner and at no time was disagreeable to the taste."[23]

The state board of forestry entertained thoughts of re-planting the smelter-denuded hills at that time but nothing ever came of the idea. Munns's suggestion that the California Debris Commission take a hand in the problem brought no response. For years thereafter the land lay wide open to sun and storm, derelict and disintegrating. In conservation propaganda of the period the California smelter area took its rightful place alongside Ducktown, Tennessee, as a prime ex-ample of the tragedy of advanced soil erosion stemming from shortsighted use and abuse of the land—"illustrating to a su-perlative degree," in the words of one Agriculture Depart-ment report, "the debt mankind owe to vegetation for its influence on surface runoff and erosion and the price we must pay when we destroy it." Public as well as scientific awareness of this singular scar on the American earth appears to have lagged remarkably, however.[24]

The 1915 eruption of nearby Lassen Peak had ruined only a fraction of the area devastated by the Shasta County smelters, and the place was declared a national park. The miles of artificial badland sprawled between Redding and Kennett far eclipsed the Lassen volcanic area and surely merited some kind of acclaim as a scenic gem-grotesque, but

[23] California Board of Forestry, *Report to the Legislature on Senate Concurrent Resolution No. 27 (Legislature of 1921)*, 25–31. And yet contemporary river surveys did not complain about any major silting or shoaling from this source: see, for example, Bailey, *The Devel-opment of the Upper Sacramento River*.
[24] California Board of Forestry, *Eighth Biennial Report*, 10–11; California Board of Forestry, *Report to Legislature on Resolution 27*, 59, 93–94; Bennett and Chapline, *Soil Ero-sion*, 16. See also Hagwood, *The California Debris Commission*.

the place was ignored quite like a bastard child. The unique legacy of a man-made desert—ghastly perfect in its barrenness, but completely lacking the balance and composure of a natural desert—appears to have inspired neither wonder nor despair in its inheritors, only a kind of dumb embarrassment. Contemporary photographs disclose the same "high hideousness close to beauty" that gripped Jonathan Daniels when he beheld the smelter desert at Ducktown; the same grim intimations of "the logical end of an undirected machine age" that troubled Stuart Chase when he visited Ducktown around the same time. The industrial wasteland of the Sacramento River canyon should have suggested more than one apt theme to talents of similar bent, but we find no thoughtful essay commemorating the place. We find barely a mention of it even in common guidebooks of the time.[25]

Likewise, the Shasta County smelter area could have supplied hydrologists, ecologists, and other natural scientists with many unique opportunities for field study, but the research potential went almost entirely unrealized. Walter Clay Lowdermilk, a famous name in American soil science, toured the area in the late 1920s and took a few photographs, but he undertook no sustained investigation of the problem and left no written comments. We find just one short paper published in 1937 by watershed scientists of the U.S. Forest Service, comparing infiltration rates on denuded land at Kennett with conditions on a nearby forested site. They found that the forest soil, with a fully developed litter cover, was able to absorb and retain at least thirteen times more rainfall than the barren ground. Their painstaking measurements only confirmed the self-evident fact that "the destruction of the forest has impaired the ability of the denuded land to absorb

---

[25] Daniels, *A Southerner Discovers the South*, 79; Chase, *Rich Land, Poor Land*, 52; Federal Writers Project, *California: A Guide to the Golden State*, 436.

precipitation, resulting in accelerated surface runoff and erosion and finally complete devastation of the area."[26]

The birth of the Central Valley Project and the approval
of plans for a crucial high dam on the Sacramento River at
Kennett brought renewed attention to the smelter area during the 1930s. The golden age of public works was at hand.
Saving the victim in the first place might have been beyond
the declared competence of traditional departments of government, but the business of doctoring the corpse now took
shape as a promising vein of funds and publicity for agencies
of recent birth. Government foresters pointed out the "grave
danger" that slipping slopes and rapid sedimentation might
pose to an expensive structure in that locality. Local cham-
ber-of-commerce types lobbied hard for their bit of the New
Deal, much the way their fathers once courted the copper
companies. Got up into something called the "Shasta-Cas-
cade Wonderland Association," Redding business leaders
told a visiting committee of congressmen how "the land no
longer has the same productive qualities or the ability to regulate stream flow." They fumbled to explain the former ob-
session with obtaining "the greatest revenue at the present
time," with "very little thought to public values."[27]

In 1933 personnel from the California Forest and Range
Experiment Station and the Civil Works Administration
staked out a characteristic tract of gullied land off the old
Mammoth Mine Road and began five years of planting and

---

[26] Walter Clay Lowdermilk papers, Bancroft Library, University of California, Berkeley; Rowe, Ilch, and Bollaert, *An Infiltration Study of a Denuded and a Forest Covered Soil*.
Compare Tennessee Valley Authority Technical Library, "Experimental Watersheds: Copper Basin [1942-51]." See also Archibold, "Vegetation Recovery Following Pollution Control at Trail, British Columbia," 1625–37; Winterhalder, "Environmental Degradation and
Rehabilitation in the Sudbury Area," 15–47; Harden, "Fluvial Response to Land-Use
Change in the Southern Appalachian Region," 407–408.

[27] U.S. Forest Service, *A National Plan for American Forestry*, vol. 1, 423; U.S. Congress,
Forest Lands of the United States, vol. 1, 940.

sowing tests in an effort to develop an effective revegetation strategy for the area. A sparse recovery of manzanita and poison oak, the only plants that seemed to thrive on these emaciated hills, had come up over much of the ground Edward Munns had classified as completely barren twelve years before. Grasses, forbs, and other tokens of a healthy soil mantle were practically nonexistent, however. An occasional volunteer pine sapling could be found here and there, but prospects for natural reforestation were anything but good. The lashing rains of twenty-odd winters already had cut and slurried away most of the topsoil with its precious capital of humus and plant nutrients. In its place a so-called erosion pavement had formed, the thick clutter of gravel and rock fragments left behind after sheet erosion whisked away the finer soil particles. Ever-widening gullies in the dull beige earth were exposing the acidic subsoil formations in gaudy shades of red and yellow. In summer the California sun beat hard on the naked slopes, making for abnormally severe surface temperatures and soil moisture losses.

The experiment station men soon gave up the effort to find a ground cover plant that would succeed on these baked, leached, rocky surfaces. Grasses, clovers, vines, and shrubs of many kinds both native and exotic were tested in different years but all plots promptly failed. Better luck was had with plantings of nursery-grown seedlings of ponderosa pine, which showed surprisingly good survival and growth on the bare ridges without mulching, fertilization, or any other prior site preparation. In the absence of an herbaceous ground cover, it was hoped that the litter mat shed by the pines as they grew and filled out would sufficiently inhibit sheet erosion and "smother" rills and gullies before they enlarged. The planting trials conducted during these years also suggested that cuttings of native arroyo willow would succeed in the

[Above] Eroded ridge west of Shasta Dam site, 1948. A fair recovery of manzanita with scattered reappearance of ponderosa pines. Elevation approximately 1,200 feet; annual rainfall approximately 60 inches.

[Below] Close-up view of gullied slope above, showing awful intensity of forty years of smelter-fume damage and storm erosion. Both photographs by A. E. McCloud. Images K-7957-CV, K-7962-CV, Photo Lab Archives, Mid-Pacific Regional Office, U.S. Bureau of Reclamation, Sacramento, California.

bottoms of established gullies, taking root as "living barriers" and forming thickets heavy enough, and hopefully doing it fast enough, to restrain further downcutting.[28]

In 1938 work began on the giant structure we know today as Shasta Dam. Nine miles downstream at Keswick a smaller companion dam was planned to provide afterbay regulation of water releases from the big reservoir. Dam construction continued through the war years but revegetation work was temporarily shelved for lack of funds and manpower. As Shasta and Keswick dams neared completion in the late 1940s, project engineers worried that sediment and debris once flushed away by the strong current of the undammed river now would start piling up in the slack water of the new reservoirs. Keswick was obviously the more threatened of the two. Charles Kraebel explained:

> Shasta Dam stands at about the middle of the denuded area, Keswick at its downstream boundary. Each reservoir, therefore, receives about half of the eroded material, but with very different effects. Shasta, with a capacity of four-and-a-half million acre-feet, can easily accommodate the debris until the area becomes naturally stabilized, with little or no effect on its performance. Keswick, a small canyon bottom reservoir of only 24,000 acre-feet, needs its full capacity to regulate the waters released from the powerhouse at Shasta Dam. Each acre-foot of sediment it receives robs Keswick of some of its effectiveness, and its dam cannot be raised because it already backs water up to the tail races of the Shasta powerhouse.[29]

A survey of the Keswick watershed was completed in 1948, and a master plan and budget for slope stabilization work was drawn up. Fifty square miles of critically eroding land—an area half again the size of San Francisco County— were mapped and scheduled for treatment. Field work began in earnest in the fall of 1949. The basic treatment strategy

---

[28] C. J. Kraebel, "Memorandum on Erosion Control in Shasta Dam Area, California," February 15, 1951, in BR 580.

[29] Kraebel, "Conquering Kennett's Gullies," 39. See also, acting district manager to construction engineer, October 20, 1950, and reply, November 13, 1950, in BR 442.

suggested by the earlier experiments was adopted—staking willow cuttings in the gullies, planting pine seedlings on the ridges between—but the engineers were afraid that rapid downward, headward, and sideward cutting by existing gully systems would likely undermine the new plantings before they could take hold. The apparent solution was "plugging" the gully channels with chains of small dams, each check serving to break the velocity of the running water, thereby letting it down the slope in easy stages and keeping its channel from gouging any deeper. Concrete and lumber structures were ruled out as impractical. "Slopes were too steep, foundations unsuitable, and the sites generally inaccessible for the delivery of such materials." Instead, the plugs were going to be made of the natural materials right at hand: loose rock where it was plentiful and cut brush where rock was lacking. By far most of the plugs would be of brush, especially on the upper slopes. Long, stiff branches of manzanita were packed lengthwise in the gullies, butt-ends pointed downstream and tops anchored in tamped earth. Again Kraebel:

> The stability of the brush plugs is inherent in their construction. . . . The innumerable stem ends and angles, thrusting against the gully banks, develop enough friction to keep the structure from sliding. Runoff water, arriving at such a barrier, is slowed down and broken into trickles instead of a free fall as it filters through the tangled brush. As the sediments drop from the slowed water, they weight and consolidate the structure. Below the barrier the water cannot develop much velocity before it strikes another plug. In a fully checked gully the water is thus stepped down slowly to a main creek or reservoir.[30]

The Keswick erosion control program was dogged from the start by swelling costs and an assortment of other problems. As work crews entered the rugged watersheds it quickly was seen that the preliminary budget of $273,000 would fall far

---

[30] Kraebel, "Conquering Kennett's Gullies," 44.

Small crew working on brush dams somewhere in Keswick watershed, 1951. Topographic and erosional conditions obviously less than promising. Photograph by J. D. Leeper. Image KE-1338-CV, Photo Lab Archives, Mid-Pacific Regional Office, U.S. Bureau of Reclamation, Sacramento, California.

short of actual needs. The initial activity in 1949–51 was
concentrated along the smaller creeks immediately below
Shasta Dam, badly cut up and degraded areas right around
the old Coram smelter site. Work that was supposed to be
accomplished for around $46,000 ended up costing over
$160,000. The original survey called for 8,500 check dams in
these drainages but over 29,000 had to be constructed; the
500,000 pine seedlings required to complete planting were
in similar high contrast to the 150,000 provided in the original schedule. Even worse topographic and erosional conditions were encountered as work progressed southward and
treatment of the Motion Creek and Gaston Gulch sections
got under way. In the crumbly country rock of these large
drainage ways, gullying in many places had advanced to
canyon-like dimensions, the little "furrows" and "wrinkles"
described so mincingly by Herbert Lang thirty years before
having expanded into slashing ditches and radiating chasms
more than fifty feet deep and hundreds of feet long.[31]

Difficulty of access was a major problem throughout the
project area, and some fifty miles of new road had to be
graded over the dissected slopes so men and material could
reach the work sites. Hand labor was and would remain the
chief item of expenditure in this costly essay in land rehabilitation. The headlong slopes around Keswick proved too
steep and rocky for efficient work even with mattocks and
shovels. A special planting tool had to be devised, a pointed
steel dibble with a foot stirrup welded on the side. This prim-
itive but effective instrument enabled planting on declivi-
ties that otherwise would have been written off as impossible.
Legal access was equally troublesome over much of the treatment area. Half the severely eroding land was still in private
ownership, complexly intermingled with what was owned by

[31] "Summary Report, Erosion Control and Stabilization, Keswick Reservoir Watershed," 1951, and construction engineer to district manager, April 9, 1951, in BR 580.

Broken ground on shoulder of Copley Mountain, draining to Motion Creek, about midway between Coram and Keswick, 1952. Photograph by J. D. Leeper. Image KE-1395-CV, Photo Lab Archives, Mid-Pacific Regional Office, U.S. Bureau of Reclamation, Sacramento, California.

the federal government. The mineral value of these tracts made purchase by the government impractical and at the same time made private owners indifferent to any improvement of surface conditions. The attitude of the Balaklala company in particular was described as "extremely belligerent" toward any reclamation. The Bureau of Reclamation was obliged to negotiate special easements to pursue the work. There was no suggestion at this time that the mining companies should be forced to contribute financially to the project. If the government had tried it no doubt would have found itself estopped by the myopic agreements it had concluded with the corporations in 1908 and 1913.[32]

---

[32] Temple, "Dawson Planting Tool," 3; construction engineer to district manager, February 1, 1950, and "Summary Report, Erosion Control and Stabilization, Keswick Reservoir and Watershed," 1951, in BR 580.

By the close of 1953 over a million pine seedlings had been planted in the Keswick reforestation scheme, with tens of thousands of pounds of acorns distributed in seed plots. In the gullies along the west side of the reservoir, 103,000 rock and brush check dams had been installed and the drainage ways planted up with 620,000 willow cuttings and 149,000 broadleaf seedlings, the species most utilized being native redbud and two tough exotics, blackleaf acacia and Spanish broom. "We feel that remarkable progress has been made," the engineers reported, but the work was still less than two-thirds done. Two years remained to finish the initial treatment of the project area, then two years more to rework it. Another million pines remained to be planted.[33]

In 1954 the initial phase of treatment on the west side watersheds was completed, and the field force was trimmed by half. Only a light treatment was scheduled for the east side of the reservoir because it was known to be more stable geologically and had a thicker covering of brush. A bulldozer was brought in to push up big earth dams along the lower reaches of Motion Creek and Gaston Gulch, but these structures did not prove substantial enough to withstand the heavy runoff of the following winter. They were filled to capacity with gravel and sediment by early spring, when unusually intense storm waters came down and channeled through the whole series. "There are no plans for further treatment of this serious erosion condition due to the prohibitive costs involved," the report laconically concluded.[34]

Half a million man-hours and money and materiel galore had been expended on Keswick soil stabilization by the close of 1957, and the end was not yet. A new cooperative pro-

[33] Supervisor of Shasta Dam Division to district manager, February 19 and March 25, 1953, and supervising engineer to chairman of California Senate Interim Committee on Public Lands, January 3, 1953, in BR 580.

[34] Supervisor of Shasta Dam Division to district manager, February 19, 1953, and C. A. Ragan to operations supervisor, June 18, 1954, in BR 580.

Gravelly wash into the new Keswick Reservoir from Motion Creek (Copley Mountain slides), 1952. Photograph by J. D. Leeper. Image KE-1400-CV, Photo Lab Archives, Mid-Pacific Regional Office, U.S. Bureau of Reclamation, Sacramento, California.

gram between the Bureau of Reclamation and the Forest Service was inaugurated in 1958, under which another million dollars of federal money would be poured into erosion control around the Keswick and Shasta reservoirs. An intensive reworking of the Keswick watersheds was undertaken over the next five years. Crews worked up and down 140 miles of gullies, raising and rebuilding old check dams and putting in new ones—over forty thousand of them. Broadleaf plantings in the ravines were extended and diversified with thousands of oleander and black locust seedlings. Replanting of pine was done wherever gaps remaining from the initial coverage were discovered, or wherever the original planting had been ruined by rodent depredations or other causes. Such failures must have been extensive, for a million

additional pine seedlings had been planted by 1962, when
the work around Keswick finally was terminated.[35]

An erosion control campaign also was started on the fume-
killed watersheds north and west of Shasta Dam. Aesthetic
amelioration was the main consideration here, and check
dam construction was kept to a minimum in order to push
pine planting. Many of the worst gully systems on the lower
slopes had been submerged by the waters of the big lake, but
some ten thousand acres were still exposed, raw and eroding.
Here again accomplishments fell behind schedule from the
start as workers encountered more difficult field conditions
and tighter budgets than anticipated. Work ended up being
confined to the lower drainage ways of Squaw and Little
Backbone creeks, areas that could be reached by existing access roads. Over two million pine seedlings were set out by
the end of 1963, but the acreage treated was not quite half
that originally projected. By then well over $600,000 had
been spent on little more than four thousand acres of ground.
Over the next four years another $200,000 in touch-up
money was coaxed out of increasingly reluctant Bureau of
Reclamation administrators.[36]

It was recognized that the continuing erosion around the
Shasta Reservoir's west shore, however appalling to the eye,
never would significantly deplete the dead storage space of
that vast lake. The situation around the Keswick reservoir
was more troubling. Erosion and sedimentation were still un-

[35] Chief of Shasta Operations Field Branch to regional supervisor of Irrigation and
Power, April 7, 1959, and April 5, 1960, and chief of Shasta Field Division, "Annual Re-
port(s) of Soil and Moisture Accomplishments," 1958–62, in BR 580.

[36] Chief of Shasta Operations Field Branch to regional supervisor of Irrigation and
Power, March 18, 1957, and April 8, 1958, soil conservationist to district ranger, July 14,
1960, forest service regional engineer to regional director of Bureau of Reclamation, December 27, 1963, acting assistant commissioner of Bureau of Reclamation to assistant secretary of Water and Power Development, February 10, 1964, and Chief of Shasta Field
Division, "Annual Report[s] of Soil and Moisture Accomplishments," 1958–66, in BR
580.

abated in three tributary drainage ways whose treatment by small-scale corrective measures had proved impossible. The worst by far was Spring Creek, whose watershed had been denuded and poisoned by the operations of the Mountain Copper Company half a century before. "Its surface was bare and lifeless, and strong sulfurous odors could be sensed at many places," one of the government engineers recalled. "Vegetation was practically absent and gullying and other evidences of soil erosion were seen everywhere." The pH values of soil samples ran below 2.0—literally sourer than lemon juice—and recent pine plantings had mostly failed to take. The amount of debris washing down was terrific. By 1960, just ten years after the filling of Keswick Dam, Spring Creek had piled up 750,000 cubic yards of silt, gravel, and cobbles at its mouth, and its delta, forty feet deep in places, completely filled a bay several hundred feet wide and half a mile long. Although most of this debris was being deposited above the reservoir's operating pool, the situation promised trouble for the future. Spring Creek runoff also was seriously degraded by poisonous acids and copper salts leached from old mines and tailings up-canyon, causing frequent trout and salmon kills in Keswick Reservoir. The Spring Creek Debris and Pollution Control Dam, a $4 million structure, two hundred feet high and eleven hundred feet across, was completed in 1963 to intercept the sediments and control releases of toxic water.[37]

---

[37] M. W. Brown, "Memorandum to the files," August 12, 1957, and chief development engineer to assistant commissioner of Bureau of Reclamation, November 19, 1959, in BR 442; Prokopovich, "Siltation and Pollution Problems in Spring Creek, Shasta County, Calif.," 986–95. The toxic mine-drainage problem proved to be most refractory and still is unresolved, but all that is another story. See, for example, California Department of Water Resources, Northern District, "Sacramento River Water Quality and Biology (Keswick Dam to Verona): A Literature Review," 5–7; *Sacramento Bee*, October 20, 2000; U.S. Environmental Protection Agency, "Abandoned Mine Lands Case Study: Iron Mountain Mine," March 7, 2006, http://www.epa.gov/aml/tech/imm.pdf.

In Keswick's other intractable tributaries, Motion Creek and Gaston Gulch, unfavorable geology and exorbitant costs ruled out high debris dams, water diversion conduits, or any other control works of a permanent character. It was decided to leave it to time and the elements to wear down the high vertical sides of these ravines to angles that would again support vegetation, even though natural stabilization would take many years and large volumes of soil would be lost in the process. "This loss will have to be accepted," one of the government foresters reported, "a sort of final payment by Society for the original mistake of having permitted the

Looking north up Sacramento River canyon from a ridge spur above Matheson, three miles north of Keswick, 1927. Sulfurous ore from Iron Mountain was brought down here by aerial tram for shipment by rail to Mountain Copper's chemical plant near Richmond on San Francisco Bay. Photograph by L. M. Correll. Image 222,692 (Quadrangle 23), Vegetation Type Analysis Photographs, Bioscience and Natural Resources Library, University of California, Berkeley.

Looking north toward Shasta Dam, six miles distant, from atop a rusting tram tower at Matheson, 2007. Though not an exact repeat of the view on page 206, this view amply illustrates the eighty-year contrast in land cover in this segment of the canyon. Scattered ponderosa pines and much volunteer manzanita, but underlying barren soil still very evident. The long-term results secured by approximately $5 million in federal reforestation expenditure, 1948–62. Photograph by Khaled J. Bloom. Author's files.

wholesale destruction of the forest cover in the first place." Downhill movement of slide material continued but it was found that the accumulation of heavy debris at the bottom tended to build up more than out, with most of the finer material carried away by the river, so interference with reservoir operation turned out to be less than originally feared. Sections and soundings taken in 1957–58 concluded that delta deposits probably would not have too adverse an impact on the reservoir after all unless they began to obstruct the channel, and if that became a problem the excess gravel deposit could be cleared from time to time by dragline. The deltas of Motion Creek and Gaston Gulch are still recognized as potential troublemakers, however, and still are being watched. A 1983 survey showed that Gaston Gulch had dumped 62,000 cubic yards of gravel and cobbles in the reservoir, Motion Creek 148,000 cubic yards. The channel had been constricted about 50 percent at both places.[38]

In 1975 the U.S. Bureau of Land Management contemplated aggressive remedial action on the six thousand or so acres in its custody in the Keswick erosion area. A reconnaissance by one of the bureau's watershed technicians soundly discouraged the idea. The government's earlier efforts had been "nearly total failures," in his verdict. He found that the thousands of check dams installed twenty years before had mostly washed away after a few years. The long-term success of tree and shrub plantings in the sour skeletal soil ranged from "only fair" to "negligible." He concluded that any further investment would be "doomed to certain failure because of the inhospitable conditions," and that rehabilitation of the land was best left to "natural processes" and to indigenous plants that were "slowly adapting to the present environmental situation." Surely the exorbitant expense of a renewed effort at this time was discouraging enough in itself. Millions of dollars had been shelled out on the government's first reforestation campaign in the California smelter area, at a time when the cost of labor in the region averaged only two dollars an hour and overall costs figured to less than $200 an acre. By the 1980s treatment costs for similar (if anything, less refractory) problem areas elsewhere in North America were quoted at over $2,000 an acre.[39]

---

[38] Chief of Shasta Operations Field Branch to regional supervisor of Irrigation and Power, May 19, 1958, in BR 442; "Memorandum to Central Files," December 28, 1983, in Chief Engineer's Working Files, U.S. Bureau of Reclamation, Shasta Dam, Calif.

[39] Russell D. Stephens, "Keswick Reservoir Watershed Survey, September, 1975," in File 7200, Redding Area Office, U.S. Bureau of Land Management, Redding, Calif.; Polk County Soil Conservation District, *A Cooperative Soil Conservation Plan for the Copper Basin, Polk County, Tennessee*; Lautenbach, "The Greening of Sudbury," 228–31.

Epilogue

So it was that widespread damage of a permanent character, never reckoned with at the appropriate time and suffered to pass almost scot-free—one of those things economists term an "external diseconomy"—was more or less internalized at long last, pecuniary and nonpecuniary costs ultimately swallowed by a taxpaying public two and three generations removed from the original conflict. A minute cost-benefit analysis possibly could show that the primary arbiters in the California smoke war—the judges who declined to punish, the officials who declined to press the issue, indeed the public who declined to protest—were right enough in their utilitarian calculus. The $100 million or so (1910 dollars) in gross product yielded by the Shasta smelters clearly overbalances $10 million or so (1960 dollars) in government reclamation expenses. On the other hand, $10 million in uncharged erosion-control and reforestation costs largely offsets the margin of investor profit that made copper smelting here attractive in the first place. On still another hand it is fair to point out that much if not most of the federal government's reclamation expenditure here was misconceived and wasted. But then again, the large-scale resource wastage it tried to correct was real and abiding, even if it is impossible to place a sure dollar value on it.

And what was the fate of the farmers and ranchers, those private property owners whose "vested interest" has been identified by some optimists as "the first line of defense against the expansion of environmental destruction"? They appear to have come off rather poorly. Shasta County agriculture bounced back nicely enough after the closing of the last copper smelter in 1919: alfalfa plantings increased more than 40 percent between 1920 and 1930, prune plantings more than 100 percent, olive plantings more than 400 percent, and the valuation of farms in the Anderson-Cottonwood and Happy Valley irrigation districts rose to over $11 million, in a decade when American agriculture generally was sadly depressed. But my examination of population schedules of the 1920 U.S. census shows that of the 205 members of the Shasta County Farmers' Protective Association in June 1910, 110 (54 percent) had vanished completely from the county by June 1920—in a decade when American agriculture generally was flourishing. I have no way of knowing how this compares with the ten-year turnover in rural communities elsewhere in the state or nation at the time, but it strikes me as remarkably high. The local papers took note when Baron W. E. J. van Balvaren sold his 685-acre hobby ranch in Shasta County and retreated to his ancestral estate in Holland in 1916. I have found nothing on the later status or whereabouts of McCoy Fitzgerald, among 107 others. I am pleased to report that Charles Paige, by far the most eloquent and interesting of the antismelter crowd, lived where he lived till 1940 and presently reposes in the old Masonic cemetery at Shasta. Paige happened to make it to age 87, but the adverse medical impact of smelter smoke on the region's inhabitants is another item of social or "external" cost that can only be surmised. Sulfur dioxide is a serious irritant to human mucous tissue, highly distressing to asthmatics and generally conducive to infections of the nose, throat, and lung. Mingled with arsenic and other elements known to have been in the Shasta ore, it has been implicated as a cofactor in cancer of the lung. But with a set of resident property owners as transitory as this, who can tell? Of the thousands of landless, nameless working stiffs who shuffled through the Shasta County smelter towns, who could possibly tell?[1]

And how about the jurist whose logic faithfully executed the wishes of the larger society that gave him office? Judge Erskine Ross rose to favor when he authorized a preemptive crackdown by southern California police and military during the 1894 Pullman Strike. He was hailed for an 1895 decision that freed Central Pacific stockholders of any liability for $60 million in defaulted federal loans, thereby saving the infant Stanford University from pending crib death. But his 1906 Mountain Copper decision likely was the most far-reaching call of his long career. It clearly overshadowed all subsequent developments in the California smoke war. It would be invoked as sound precedent in analogous cases all over the American West, notably a 1908 decision by Ross himself that authorized the gross pollution of Idaho's Coeur d'Alene River. The latter resulted in what is today the U.S. Environmental Protection Agency's second-costliest toxic cleanup challenge west of the Rockies—the costliest being the old Iron Mountain copper mine, Shasta County, California. In 1909 the state bar association and many California newspapers pushed Judge Ross for elevation to the U.S. Supreme Court, and it generally was agreed he would have

---

[1] Goldman, *The Spoils of Progress*, 73–75; U.S. Census, *Fifteenth Census, 1930: Irrigation of Agricultural Lands*, 370, 372, 376; Shasta County manuscript schedules for population, Fourteenth U.S. Census, 1920, National Archives Microfilm Publication T625, roll 127; *Redding Courier-Free Press*, April 20, 1916; Shasta County cemetery records, Shasta Historical Society, Redding, Calif.

made it had he not been a former Confederate army officer, at a time when the White House and Senate were firmly in the hands of second-generation Republicans. Meanwhile he made a small fortune in real estate in the San Gabriel Valley east of Los Angeles, where there were no mines or smelters, nor hardly a wisp of smog as yet. Judge Ross was injured in a traffic accident in his elder years and afterward was tortured by what was courteously described as "muscular impairment." A goat-testicle implant performed by a celebrated Kansas quack did nothing to stay his decline. He retired from the federal bench in 1925 and was buried in 1928 with the usual panegyrics. Calvin Coolidge praised his "high qualities of learning, wisdom, moderation, and great firmness."[2]

---

[2] Cosgrave, *Early California Justice*, 67–72; "McCarthy et al. v. Bunker Hill and Sullivan Mining and Concentrating Company et al.," 940–41; Aiken, *Idaho's Bunker Hill*, 63–65, 110–14; *San Francisco Call*, November 11, 1909; *San Francisco Examiner*, April 20, 1922; *San Francisco Chronicle*, April 10, 1925. See also National Research Council, *Superfund and Mining Megasites*, 22–46; Carson, *The Roguish World of Doctor Brinkley*, 46–48.

Bibliography
and Index

Bibliography

ARCHIVAL SOURCES

California Attorney General. Letter Books, 1906–1941. California State Archives, Sacramento, Calif.

California Board of Health. Secretary's Log, 1914–1922. California State Archives, Sacramento, Calif.

California Supreme Court, Sacramento District. Civil Case File 1847. California State Archives, Sacramento, Calif.

Shasta County Superior Court. Civil Case File 3120. Shasta County Clerk, Redding, Calif.

Shasta Historical Society. Historical Photograph Collection. Redding , Calif.

Solano County Superior Court. Civil Case Files 2980, 3017, 3074, and 3090. Solano County Archives, Fairfield, Calif.

U.S. Bureau of Land Management. Historical File 7200. Redding, Calif.

U.S. Bureau of Reclamation. Central File 442: Research, Testing and Technical Miscellany: Sedimentation. Shasta Dam, Calif.

———. Central File 580: Keswick Reservoir Watersheds: April 1951–December 1957. Shasta Dam, Calif.

U.S. Circuit Court of Appeals, Eighth Circuit. Civil Case File 2549. Record Group 276, National Archives, Kansas City, Mo.

U.S. Circuit Court of Appeals, Ninth Circuit. Civil Case Files 1203 and 1738. Record Group 276, National Archives, San Bruno, Calif.

U.S. Department of Interior, Lands and Railroads Division. Letters Received File 5154–1897. Record Group 48, National Archives, College Park, Md.

U.S. Department of Justice. Year File 5706–1898. Record Group 60, National Archives, College Park, Md.

————. Straight Numerical File 144276. Record Group 60, National Archives, College Park, Md.

U.S. District Court, Northern District of California. Civil Case Files 12633, 15122, 15123, 15798, 15818, 15820, and 15837, and Equity Case Files 250 and 251. Record Group 21, National Archives, San Bruno, Calif.

U.S. Forest Service. Research Compilation File: Smelter Fumes. Record Group 95, National Archives, College Park, Md.

————. Pacific Southwest Forest and Range Experiment Station. Photographs and Research Data. Federal Records Center, San Bruno, Calif.

U.S. General Land Office, Special Services Division. California Timber Trespass Case File 30. Record Group 49, National Archives, College Park, Md.

————. Division P. Case File 55979. Record Group 49, National Archives, College Park, Md.

University of California, Bancroft Library. Office of University President papers, George Pardee papers, Hiram Johnson papers, Walter Lowdermilk papers, and Charles Kraebel papers. Berkeley, Calif.

————. Bioscience and Natural Resources Library. Vegetation Type Analysis Photographs. Berkeley, Calif.

GOVERNMENT DOCUMENTS

Aubury, Lewis E. *The Copper Resources of California.* California State Mining Bureau Bulletin 50. Sacramento: State Printer, 1908.

Bailey, Paul. *The Development of the Upper Sacramento River.* California Division of Engineering and Irrigation Bulletin 13. Sacramento: State Printer, 1928.

Bennett, H. H., and W. R. Chapline. *Soil Erosion: A National Menace*. U.S. Department of Agriculture Circular 33. Washington, D.C.: Government Printing Office, 1928.

California Air Resources Board. "A Joint Study of Lead Contamination Relative to Horse Deaths in Southern Solano County." Sacramento, 1972.

California Board of Forestry. *Eighth Biennial Report*. Sacramento: State Printer, 1921.

———. *Report to the Legislature on Senate Concurrent Resolution No. 27 (Legislature of 1921)*, Sacramento: State Printer, 1923.

California Board of Health. *Report for 1906–1908*. Sacramento: State Printer, 1908.

California Department of Water Resources. "Sacramento River Water Quality and Biology (Keswick Dam to Verona): A Literature Review." Chico, Calif., 1986.

California Legislature. *Final Calendar of Legislative Business, Fortieth Session, 1913*. Sacramento: State Printer, 1913.

Clar, C. Raymond. *California Government and Forestry, from Spanish Days until the creation of the Department of Natural Resources in 1927*. Sacramento: California Division of Forestry, 1959.

Griffin, James R., and W. R. Critchfield. *The Distribution of Forest Trees in California*, U.S. Forest Service Forest Research Paper PSW-82. Berkeley: Pacific Southwest Forest and Range Experiment Station, 1976.

Hagwood, Joseph J., Jr. *The California Debris Commission: a history of the hydraulic ming industry of the western Sierra Nevada and of the governmental agency charged with its regulation*. Sacramento: U.S. Army Corps of Engineers, 1981.

Haywood, J. K. *Injury to Vegetation by Smelter Fumes*. U.S. Bureau of Chemistry Bulletin 89. Washington, D.C.: Government Printing Office, 1905.

———. *Injury to Vegetation and Animal Life by Smelter Wastes*. U.S. Bureau of Chemistry Bulletin 113. Washington, D.C.: Government Printing Office, 1910.

Holmes, J. A., Edward C. Franklin, and Ralph A. Gould. *Report of the Selby Smelter Commission.* U.S. Bureau of Mines Bulletin 98. Washington, D.C.: Government Printing Office, 1915.

Kinkel, A.R., Jr., W. E. Hall, and J. P. Albers. *Geology and Base-Metal Deposits of the West Shasta Copper-Zinc District, California.* U.S. Geological Survey Professional Paper 285. Washington, D.C., 1956.

Lapham, Macy C., and L. C. Holmes. *Soil Survey of the Redding Area, California.* Washington, D.C., Government Printing Office, 1908.

Merchant, James A., ed. *Occupational Respiratory Diseases.* National Institute for Occupational Safety and Health Publication 86-102. Washington, D.C.: Government Printer, 1986.

Metzger, G. K. *Trail Smelter Reference: Brief for the Government of the United States Submitted to the International Joint Commission.* U.S. Department of State Publication 71. Washington, D.C.: Government Printer, 1930.

Polk County Soil Conservation District. *A Cooperative Soil Conservation Plan for the Copper Basin, Polk County, Tennessee.* Benton, Tenn., 1987.

Rowe, P. B., D. M. Ilch, and René Bollaert. *An Infiltration Study of a Denuded and a Forest Covered Soil.* California Forest and Range Experiment Station Research Note 14. Berkeley, 1937.

Scheffer, Theodore C., and George G. Hedgcock. *Injury to Northwestern Forest Trees by Sulfur Dioxide from Smelters.* U.S. Department of Agriculture Technical Bulletin 1117. Washington, D.C.: Government Printing Office, 1955.

Tennessee Valley Authority Technical Library. "Experimental Watersheds: Copper Basin." Knoxville, 1983.

U.S. Bureau of Animal Industry. *Report for 1908.* Washington, D.C.: Government Printing Office, 1910.

U.S. Bureau of the Census. *Eleventh Census, 1890: Agriculture.* Washington, D.C.: Government Printing Office, 1895.

———. *Thirteenth Census, 1910: Agriculture.* Washington, D.C.: Government Printing Office, 1913.

———. *Fifteenth Census, 1930: Irrigation of Agricultural Lands.* Washington, D.C.: Government Printing Office, 1932.

U.S. Congress. *Forest Lands of the United States: Hearings before the Joint Committee on Forestry.* 76th Cong. 3 sess. 2 vols. Washington, D.C.: Government Printing Office, 1940.

———. *Hearings before a Subcommittee of the Committee on Interior and Insular Affairs.* 80th Cong. 2 sess., February 18 and 19, 1948. Washington, D.C.: Government Printing Office, 1948.

U.S. Environmental Protection Agency. "Abandoned Mine Lands Case Study: Iron Mountain Mine." 2002. Online at www.epa.gov.

U.S. Forest Service. *A National Plan for American Forestry.* 2 vols. Washington, D.C.: Government Printing Office, 1933.

COURT CASES

"American Smelting and Refining Co. et al. v. Godfrey et al." *Federal Reporter* 158 (1908).

"Appeal of the Pennsylvania Lead Company." *Pennsylvania State Reports* 96 (1883).

"Bliss v. Washoe Copper Co. et al." *Federal Reporter* 186 (1911).

"Georgia v. Tennessee Copper Company." *United States Reports* 206 (1907).

"Madison et al. v. Ducktown Sulphur, Iron, and Copper Company, etc." *Southwestern Reporter* 83 (1905).

"Mountain Copper Company, Limited, v. United States." *Federal Reporter* 142 (1906).

"People of the State of California v. Selby Smelting and Lead Company." *California Reports* 163 (1913).

"The Pennsylvania Coal Company, versus Sanderson and Wife." *Pennsylvania State Reports* 113 (1887).

"Woodruff v. North Bloomfield Gravel Mining Co., and others." *Federal Reporter* 18 (1884).

NEWSPAPERS AND PERIODICALS

Anderson Valley News, 1916

Benicia Herald, 1906–1913, 1970–1971

Copper Handbook (New York), 1906–1911

Mining and Engineering Journal (New York), 1899–1924

Mining and Scientific Press (San Francisco), 1898–1920

Mining Reporter (Denver), 1905–1914

Mining World / Mining and Engineering World (Chicago), 1905–1916

Pacific Coast Miner (San Francisco), 1897–1903

Red Bluff Daily News, 1909

Redding Courier-Free Press, 1906–1919

Redding Free Press, 1898, 1901–1906

Redding Mineral Wealth, 1900–1907

Redding Searchlight, 1898, 1901–1915

Sacramento Bee, 2000

San Francisco Call, 1876, 1898–1904

San Francisco Chronicle, 1903–1941, 1970

Shasta Weekly Courier, 1898

Transactions, Commonwealth Club of California (San Francisco), 1912–1913

BOOKS AND MONOGRAPH

Aiken, Katherine G. *Idaho's Bunker Hill: The Rise and Fall of a Great Mining Company, 1885–1981.* Norman: University of Oklahoma Press, 2005.

Ashby, Eric, and Mary Anderson. *The Politics of Clean Air.* Oxford: Clarendon Press, 1981.

Avery, David. *Not on Queen Victoria's Birthday: The Story of the Rio Tinto Mines.* London: Collins, 1974.

Barr, John. *Derelict Britain.* Harmondsworth, U.K.: Penguin Books, 1969.

Baruch, Bernard M. *Baruch: My Own Story*. New York: Henry Holt, 1957.

Bean, Walton. *Boss Ruef's San Francisco: The Story of the Union Labor Party, Big Business, and the Graft Prosecution*. Berkeley: University of California Press, 1952.

Bentley, Arthur F. *The Process of Government: A Study of Social Pressures*. Chicago: University of Chicago Press, 1908.

Blackstone, William. *Commentaries on the Laws of England: Book the Third*. Oxford: Clarendon Press, 1768.

Brechin, Gray. *Imperial San Francisco: Urban Power, Earthly Ruin*. Berkeley: University of California Press, 1999.

Bryn Mawr College Library, Special Collections. "Susan Walker FitzGerald Papers: Description of Collection." Bryn Mawr, Penn.

Carson, Gerald. *The Roguish World of Doctor Brinkley*. New York: Holt-Rinehart-Winston, 1960.

Chase, Stuart. *Rich Land, Poor Land: A Study of Waste in the Natural Resources of America*. New York: McGraw-Hill, 1936.

Cosgrave, George. *Early California Justice: The Story of the United States District Court for the Southern District of California, 1848–1944*. San Francisco: Grabhorn Press, 1948.

Cronise, Titus Fey. *The Natural Wealth of California*. San Francisco: H. H. Bancroft, 1868.

Daniels, Jonathan. *A Southerner Discovers the South*. New York: Macmillan, 1938.

Davenport, W. G., M. King, M. Schlesinger, and A. K. Biswas. *Extractive Metallurgy of Copper*. 4th ed. Oxford: Elsevier Science, 2002.

De Nevers, Noel. *Air Pollution Control Engineering*. New York: McGraw-Hill, 1995.

Deering, James H., ed. *The Civil Code of the State of California*. San Francisco: Bancroft-Whitney, 1909.

Dillon, Richard. *Great Expectations: The Story of Benicia, California*. Benicia, Calif.: Benicia Heritage Book, 1980.

Federal Writers Project. *California: A Guide to the Golden State.* New York: Hastings House, 1939.

Flamant, Maurice, and Jeanne Singer-Kárel. *Modern Economic Crises.* London: Barrie & Jenkins, 1970.

Frederick, David C. *Rugged Justice: The Ninth Circuit Court of Appeals and the American West, 1891–1941.* Berkeley: University of California Press, 1994.

Freyfogle, Eric G. *The Land We Share: Private Property and the Common Good.* Washington, D.C.: Island Press, 2003.

Goldman, Marshall I. *The Spoils of Progress: Environmental Pollution in the Soviet Union.* Cambridge, Mass.: MIT Press, 1972.

Grant-Francis, George. *The Smelting of Copper in the Swansea District.* 2nd ed. London: H. Sotheran, 1881.

Hacker, Louis M., Rudolf Modley, and George R. Taylor. *The United States: A Graphic History.* New York: Modern Age Books, 1937.

Hays, Samuel P. *Conservation and the Gospel of Efficiency: The Progressive Conservation Movement, 1890–1920.* Cambridge, Mass.: Harvard University Press, 1959.

Herfindahl, Orris C. *Copper Costs and Prices, 1870–1957.* Baltimore: Johns Hopkins Press, 1959.

Hichborn, Franklin. *Story of the Session of the California Legislature of 1913.* San Francisco: James H. Barry, 1913.

Hofman, H. O. *Metallurgy of Copper.* New York: McGraw-Hill, 1914.

Horwitz, Morton J. *The Transformation of American Law, 1780–1860.* Cambridge, Mass.: Harvard University Press, 1977.

Hughes, Charles E., and Timpanogos Research Associates. "United States Smelting, Refining, and Mining Company: Corporate Records Inventory." Midvale, Utah, 1991.

Hurst, James Willard. *Law and the Conditions of Freedom in the Nineteenth-Century United States.* Madison: University of Wisconsin Press, 1956.

Ise, John. *The United States Forest Policy*. New Haven, Conn.: Yale University Press, 1920.

Kelley, Robert L. *Gold vs. Grain: The Hydraulic Mining Controversy in California's Sacramento Valley*. Glendale, Calif.: Arthur H. Clark, 1959.

Kelley, Robert. *Battling the Inland Sea: American Political Culture, Public Policy, and the Sacramento Valley, 1850–1966*. Berkeley: University of California Press, 1989.

Kolko, Gabriel. *The Triumph of Conservatism: A Reinterpretation of American Politics, 1900–1916*. New York: Free Press of Glencoe, 1963.

Lavender, Stephen J. *New Land for Old: The Environmental Renaissance of the Lower Swansea Valley*. Bristol, U.K.: A. Hilger, 1981.

Limbaugh, Ronald H. and Willard P. Fuller, Jr. *Calaveras Gold: The Impact of Mining on a Mother Lode County*. Reno: University of Nevada Press, 2004.

MacMillan, Donald. *Smoke Wars: Anaconda Copper, Montana Air Pollution, and the Courts, 1890-1924*. Helena: Montana Historical Society Press, 2000.

Marcosson, Isaac F. *Metal Magic: The Story of the American Smelting & Refining Company*. New York: Farrar, Straus, 1949.

Mowry, George E. *The California Progressives*. Berkeley: University of California Press, 1951.

Murphy, Jerre C. *The Comical History of Montana: A Serious Story for Free People*. San Diego: E. L. Scofield, 1912.

Mylar, Isaac L. *Early Days at the Mission San Juan Bautista*. Watsonville, Calif.: Evening Pajaronian, 1929.

National Research Council. *Sulfur Oxides*. Washington, D.C.: National Academy of Sciences, 1978.

———. *Superfund and Mining Megasites: Lessons from the Couer d'Alene River Basin*. Washington, D.C.: National Academies Press, 2001.

Olin, Spencer C., Jr. *California's Prodigal Sons: Hiram Johnson and the Progressives, 1911–1917*. Berkeley: University of California Press, 1968.

Orsi, Richard J. *Sunset Limited: The Southern Pacific Railroad Company and the Development of the American West, 1850–1930*. Berkeley: University of California Press, 2005.

Percival, Robert V., Alan S. Miller, Christopher S. Schroeder, and James P. Leape. *Environmental Regulation: Law, Science, and Policy*. Boston: Little, Brown, 1992.

Rees, Ronald. *King Copper: South Wales and the Copper Trade, 1584–1895*. Cardiff: University of Wales Press, 2000.

Rice, Richard B., William A. Bullough, and Richard J. Orsi. *The Elusive Eden: A New History of California*. 2nd ed. New York: McGraw-Hill, 1996.

Stadtman, Verne A. *The University of California, 1868–1968: A Centennial Publication of the University of California*. New York: McGraw-Hill, 1970.

Stern, Arthur C., ed. *Air Pollution*. 3rd ed. 8 vols. New York: Academic Press, 1976–1986.

Stradling, David. *Smokestacks and Progressives: Environmentalists, Engineers, and Air Quality in America, 1881–1951*. Baltimore: Johns Hopkins University Press, 1999.

Veblen, Thorstein. *Absentee Ownership and Business Enterprise in Recent Times: The Case of America*. New York: B. W. Huebsch, 1923.

White, Gerald T. *Formative Years in the Far West: A History of the Standard Oil Company of California, and Predecessors through 1919*. New York: Appleton-Century-Crofts, 1962.

Winner, William E., Harold A. Mooney, and Robert A. Goldsmith, eds. *Sulfur Dioxide and Vegetation: Physiology, Ecology, and Policy Issues*. Stanford: Stanford University Press, 1986.

Wirth, John D. *Smelter Smoke in North America: The Politics of Transborder Pollution* Lawrence: University Press of Kansas, 2000.

Wood, H. G. *A Practical Treatise on the Law of Nuisances in Their Various Forms, Including Remedies therefor at Law and Equity.* 3rd ed. 2 vols. San Francisco: Bancroft-Whitney, 1893.

Zimmerman, Erich W. *World Resources and Industries.* New York: Harper & Bros., 1933.

ARTICLES

Archibold, O. W. "Vegetation Recovery Following Pollution Control at Trail, British Columbia." *Canadian Journal of Botany* 56 (1978).

Austin, W. L. "Mining Investment Values." *Mines and Methods* 3 (1911).

Baer, C. S. III, and S. B. McLaughlin. "Trace Elements in Tree Rings: Evidence of Recent and Historical Pollution." *Science* 204 (1984).

Bloom, Khaled J., and Conrad J. Bahre. "Historical Evidence for the Upslope Retreat of Ponderosa Pine in California's Gold Country." *Yearbook of the Association of Pacific Coast Geographers* 65 (2003).

Brenner, Joel Franklin. "Nuisance Law and the Industrial Revolution." *Journal of Legal Studies* 3 (1974).

Burton, R. G., and Taft Reed. "Smelter Fumes and Damage Suits." *Metallurgical and Chemical Engineering* 8 (1910).

Clay, Grady. "Copper Basin Cover-up." *Landscape Architecture* 73 (1983).

Coase, R. H. "The Problem of Social Cost." *Journal of Law and Economics* 3 (1960).

Cottrell, F. G. "The Electrical Precipitation of Suspended Particles." *Journal of Industrial and Chemical Engineering* 3 (1911).

Eddy, L. H. "What Has Been the Fume Damage in California?" *Engineering and Mining Journal* 96 (1913).

Harden, Carol P. "Fluvial Response to Land-Use Change in the Southern Appalachian Region: A Century of Investigation." *Physical Geography* 25 (2004).

Harkins, W. D., and R. D. Swain. "The Determination of Arsenic and Other Solid Constituents of Smelter Smoke, with a Study of the Effects of High Stacks and Large Condensing Flues." *Journal of the American Chemical Society* 29 (1907).

Hart, Joseph R. "Problems in the Utilization of Smelter Fumes." *Mining World* 30 (1909).

Johnson, Ligon. "History and Legal Phases of the Smelting-Smoke Problem—II." *Engineering and Mining Journal* 103 (1917).

Kett, William F. "Fifty Years of Operation by the Mountain Copper Company, Ltd., in Shasta County, California." *California Journal of Mining and Geology* 43 (1947).

Kraebel, Charles J. "Conquering Kennett's Gullies." *American Forests* 61 (1955).

Lamborn, John E., and Charles S. Peterson. "The Substance of the Land: Agriculture v. Industry in the Smelter Cases of 1904 and 1906." *Utah Historical Quarterly* 35 (1985).

Lang, Herbert. "Common Sense of the Fume Question." *Mining and Scientific Press* 107 (1913).

———. "A Metallurgical Journey to Shasta, California—V." *Mining and Scientific Press* 119 (1919).

Lautenbach, William E. "The Greening of Sudbury." *Journal of Soil and Water Conservation* 42 (1987).

LeCain, Timothy. "The Limits of 'Eco-Efficiency': Arsenic Pollution and the Cottrell Electrical Precipitator in the U.S. Copper Smelting Industry." *Environmental History* 5 (2000).

Lowden, Spencer E. "Life at the Mammoth Mine, 1907–1918." *Covered Wagon* (1977), 37.

Martin, Al. H. "The Mammoth Smelter at Kennett, California." *Mining Science* 58 (1908).

———. "The Balaklala Mine and Smelter, California." *Mining World* 32 (1910).

———. "The Balaklala Smelter and Cottrell Fume Controller." *Mining Science* 63 (1911).

Neilson, Thomas. "Roasting Copper Ore at Keswick, California." *Engineering and Mining Journal* 68 (1899).

Nevius, J. Nelson. "Shasta County Smelter-Fume Problems." *Mining and Scientific Press* 106 (1913).

Paige, Charles L. "A Complaint from Shasta." *Sacramento Record-Union*, July 30, 1897.

———. "Devastation at Keswick." *Sacramento Record-Union*, August 15, 1898.

Pisani, Donald J. "Enterprise and Equity: A Critique of Western Water Law in the Nineteenth Century." *Western Historical Quarterly* 18 (1987).

Prokopovitch, Nicola P. "Siltation and Pollution Problems in Spring Creek, Shasta County, Calif." *Journal of the American Water Works Association* 57 (1965).

Pool, Raymond J. "Forty Years on the Nebraska National Forest." *Nebraska History* 34 (1953).

Rice, Claude T. "Handling Copper Smeltery Gases." *Engineering and Mining Journal* 91 (1911).

Robbins, William G. "The 'Plundered Province' Thesis and the Recent Historiography of the American West." *Pacific Historical Review* 55 (1986).

Rose-Soley, J. F. "Sulphurous Fumes Devastate Shasta County." *San Francisco Call*, August 22, 1898.

Scheiber, Harry N. "Property Law, Expropriation, and Resource Allocation by Government: The United States, 1789–1910." *Journal of Economic History* 33 (1973).

Teale, Edwin Way. "The Murder of a Landscape." *Natural History* 60 (1951).

Topper, C. A. "Copper Smelting at the Kennett Plant, California." *Mining and Engineering World* 36 (1912).

Weldon, Geo. P. "Smelter Fumes Injury to Vegetation." *Monthly Bulletin of the California State Commission of Horticulture* 4 (1915).

Wierum, H. F. "Experimental Development of the Hall Process." *Mining and Scientific Press* 109 (1914).

Winterhalder, Keith. "Environmental Degradation and Rehabilitation in the Sudbury Area." *Laurentian University Review* 16 (1984).

Index